TRANQUEBAR

By the same author

IN ANOTHER EUROPE: A Journey to Romania

TRANQUEBAR

A Season in South India

Georgina Harding

Hodder & Stoughton

LONDON SYDNEY AUCKLAND

British Library Cataloguing in Publication Data

Harding, Georgina
  Tranquebar
  I. Title
  823.914 [F]

  ISBN 0-340-54904-1

Published by Hodder and Stoughton,
a division of Hodder and Stoughton Ltd,
Mill Road, Dunton Green, Sevenoaks, Kent TN13 2YA
Editorial Office: 47 Bedford Square, London WC1B 3DP

Photoset by Rowland Phototypesetting Ltd,
Bury St Edmunds, Suffolk

Printed in Great Britain by St Edmundsbury Press Ltd,
Bury St Edmunds, Suffolk

For Tom

CONTENTS

LONDON

Matthew Maguire lived in a clean block of 1950s flats above a row of shops in Ealing. The entrance, reached up a flight of metal stairs from a side-street, had the geranium calm of homes reserved for the borough's senior citizens. The Maguires' was lined with pot plants from porch to sitting-room, warm as a greenhouse within the double glazing.

Matthew was one of the last generation of Anglo-Indians raised under the British Empire. More precisely, he was Irish-Indian, for his paternal ancestor came from Cork, a volunteer signed up in the 1820s for the East India Company army at Madras. Matthew's father, like so many of his kind, worked on the railways, and he grew up in a railway town, Perambur, on the edge of Madras. Most of the names on the street where he lived were Irish: Murphy, Reilly, O'Connor, lettered on the gateposts, and he picked up from his parents and grandparents, and from the men who talked on the doorsteps, a soft touch of brogue. At the outbreak of the Second World War, he was old enough to serve in the British Army. When the war ended he went home and stayed on a while after Independence. In a decade he saw most of his relations and friends leave India, dispersing mainly to Australia and Canada. Eventually he left also, transferring to the London mother-office of the company he worked for, which manufactured precision instruments.

'When I was a boy we took an annual holiday at Vailankanni. A fishing village it was, seven miles south of Nagapattinam, and the shrine of Our Lady of Health. An overnight journey from Madras, the sleeping carriages being transferred at Mayuram Junction. And on the platform at Mayuram I read the sign: *Change here for Tranquebar*. I would spell out the name and try its sound. I must have heard someone mention about my great-uncle being associated with the place – Uncle Tom Ballard, my grandmother's brother, of interest

11

to me as he was something of a black sheep – but it wasn't that alone. I think it was the word itself.'

His wife brought tea and a plate of triangular white sandwiches that overlapped like petals. Linda was darker than her husband, Luso-Indian in her origin, for the Portuguese and Irish had allied, fellow Catholics, within the Eurasian community. Matthew's mixture of race showed in his build rather than his colour. He had the Tamil slightness and grace, and the fine, small features.

'I loved that journey to Vailankanni – dozing as the train clacked through the darkness, not wanting to go right off to sleep for what I'd miss. Mayuram Junction had you wide awake in a second. Always a hubbub. Cries and light and crowds. The jolt as our carriages were taken from the train, more jolts as they were coupled to the second engine. I'd watch from the window. You could lean right out in those days. That was long before they put the bars across the windows of the trains to keep the mob from climbing in.

'I don't know whether I thought I would ever go to Tranquebar. But later, when I went back to India from England, went back to discover the country long after I'd left it, Tranquebar was high on my list. I knew a bit about the place by then. I wonder if the original magic in the name wasn't the hint of its history? The first bit comes from the Tamil, given a European pronunciation; but isn't there some Arabic in the ending – like Zanzibar, Malabar, Nicobar, places that were frequented by Arab traders before ever the Europeans came to the Indian Ocean?'

His talk was dense with footnotes. He had spent many of the long days of retirement in libraries, reading up on the places that interested him. Now he would rest his hands fingertip to fingertip and tell you snippets of the history of colonial district centres with leafy maidans and railway yards and crowded British cemeteries. Every two or three years, when he had saved the money, he went back to southern India. He travelled the lines on which his relatives had worked, listed gravestones and collected friends. It was not a simple search for roots. He made it sound an historical exercise: he was recording the things which the Indians would not think to record, at least until they had quite crumbled away.

Tranquebar was a special enthusiasm. He had taken its history

12

back to colonial beginnings, though it was originally a possession of Denmark, not of Britain, and did not pass into British hands until 1845. He brought out two faded blue volumes of a publication by the Hakluyt Society, *The Life of Jon Olafsson, Traveller to India*. It was the autobiography of an Icelandic seaman in the service of the Danes who lived at Tranquebar in 1623, just three years after the colony was founded. Olafsson reported what his messmates had told him of the first Danish voyage to the Indies, which had been bound originally for the Coromandel Coast but redirected towards Ceylon, and ended where it did pretty much by chance.

Matthew relished the oddities in Olafsson's account. There was the story of the Dutchman, Marcelis de Boshouwer, who had persuaded the newly founded Danish East India Company to try Ceylon. He presented himself in Copenhagen as an envoy from the Raja of Kandy, styling himself Prince of Migomuwe, wearing exotic clothes and trailing a native servant, so convincing that the Danish king stood godfather to his son. He died on board ship just as the fleet reached Ceylon, to discover that the offer he had so impressively extended was not to be backed up by the Raja.

Then there was the puzzle of Erik Grubbe, one of the officers on the voyage. He was a nobleman and a romantic figure: his mistress had tried to join the ship dressed as a man but was soon discovered and they were married at sea off Elsinore. She and their newborn baby died somewhere on the Indian Ocean and at Ceylon Grubbe reportedly went native. Danish sailors said he spent the next few years half-mad with grief and roaming the jungle behind Trincomalee. When their ships passed they would fire three guns as a signal and he sent a boy down to the shore to collect their gifts of victuals and linen shirts. But his activities may have been more deliberate than they seemed. In Ceylon he had coins struck and inscribed with his name prefaced by the Portuguese title Don. And when at last he reappeared in Denmark he was quite sane.

Matthew Maguire thought him suspect. 'They were a disreputable lot, the Europeans who came out to Tranquebar. Pirates and con men, most of them. Excluding the missionaries of course. Some of them no doubt were saints.'

*   *   *

I had visited Tranquebar ten years earlier and I too was haunted by the place. I had been introduced to the Maguires because I was planning to spend the winter there. It must have been September by then and the idea had begun as a fantasy in the spring. I had been feeling trapped in London. I was mother of a baby boy whose squawls bounced between the walls of a terraced house. It was a fifteen-minute walk to the park, a dull stroll between grey houses and through waves of diesel fumes. I dreamt of freedom from buggies and supermarket trolleys. I would rediscover my mobility. I might even find gentle childcare and have time to write. My son Tom would learn to walk barefoot, to play without his junk-heap of plastic toys, and exclaim at elephants instead of police cars.

I made the idea firmer by telling those friends who seemed least likely to be shocked. Then I wrote letters to the three Christian churches I knew of at Tranquebar, asking for accommodation, working on the logic that the churches were likely to have experience of Westerners and that vicars in small places generally know what's going on. I would have been content to receive no reply. But the first came a fortnight later – almost by return since the post took a week each way. It was from Reverend I. G. Thambiah of the New Jerusalem Church: 'I have noted your request. Please come over here for your research. I will help you by arranging a house with all facilities. Don't worry.' A second came a week after that, from the principal of St Theresa's Training School for Girls. Sister Nirmala wrote in more detail. There was indeed a 'decent house with all facilities' newly built and available from November. The rent was 350 rupees a month. That was ten pounds. It cost another ten pounds to send the landlord a banker's draft for the first month's rent.

So, we were committed. Tom's father said he would come and see us settled in. And I began to worry. I had spent a mere half day in the place before, and then I had been a hardened traveller with no one but myself to think of. How would it be with a child?

The Maguires had both stayed at Tranquebar once, and Matthew had been back on at least a couple of occasions since. I asked them what I would be likely to find.

'A lot of dust,' said Linda. 'You'll have to see that your floor's swept twice a day. You'll need to filter and boil the water. But you

14

can get powdered milk and porridge oats. Britannia biscuits are very good and the doctors are well trained and they have antibiotics like everywhere else.' Her expression was hard to read. The Maguires had one son, grown up now and a musician in a rock band. Would she have done the same with him?

Matthew was enthusiastic. He said Linda had never been one to travel rough. He gave me the names of the Roman Catholic priest and a friendly pharmacist in the local town.

THE COLONY

The heathen king lent [us, for] our king, a pleasant and smooth place by the sea . . .

Jon Olafsson

1

I remembered King Street as white, a white street open to the sea. When I returned I saw that most of the houses were yellow, the colour burnt like that of the ground across which their shadows fell. On the south side, on the right as you enter the village, almost all the houses are the same dull ochre, save the little grocery just past the town gate (selling spices and grains, toffees, Surf and Palmolive) which has walls washed a strong turquoise, and the Lutheran church, restored in minty shades of green. The image must have come from the few white buildings on the south side: St Theresa's teacher training college, once the residence of Danish governors, dazzling beneath the sun at midday; and the two houses of the Nadars. The first of these stands next to the training college, long and neoclassical. The second, right at the end facing on to the old parade ground, is known as the seashore bungalow, set in a garden of palms that is crumbling into the sea.

That first visit I made to Tranquebar was in May or June, at the height of the hot weather, but on an overcast day when the wind fretted at the hard leaves of tropical trees. I came by train on the metre-gauge branch line that ran the thirty kilometres from Mayuram Junction. There can have been no more than three or four carriages and I remember no other passengers. Yet there must have been some in the other compartments, since at one station a grimy young girl appeared by the track and worked down the length of the train performing an awkward song and dance routine. She reeled off her words in a high, unvarying pitch and raced mechanically through her steps, watching for paise coins in the dust. At the stationmaster's whistle she had reached my window, and she accelerated to the end of the dance like an overwound clockwork doll.

Tranquebar was the end of the line. The station stood alone in a bare stretch of fields by a rivermouth. A track led up to a metalled road on an embankment and from there a strip of beach showed beyond the mudflat. To the left of this lay the fort like a stranded battleship, and further along, the tip of a church tower stood above some trees. After a few hundred metres the road bridged the river and entered a row of shuttered shops, and from there the Danish Landgate led into the village. This was a deep baroque archway. Once it would have been plastered to look like stone but thin red brick showed now through phantom pilasters and rustications; more plaster decoration remained on the pediments, between the ornamental piles of cannonballs, revealing the Danish royal arms on the inland face and on the seaward side the date 1792.

Running directly ahead was King Street. The time must have been near noon and the sun shot the haze through with its glare. The street was empty. I walked past the colonial buildings with their pillars and locked doors and found the Lutheran church, standing in a packed graveyard behind iron gates and a line of mast trees in glossy imitation of cypress. Inside, the breeze was no longer fretful but cooling; the cruciform plan of the church conjured in a draught through windows on all sides. The open shutters framed a lush view of leaves and bougainvillea; within were white walls, polished pews and pulpit, northern and puritanical. Further down the street on the opposite side was a second Christian church, the one whose tower had shown in the distance. But the Zion Church was blanketed in dust and registers lay disintegrating on the vestry shelves.

There was no one about, no shop open, no tea stall. I had water but nothing to eat. The old parade ground was a wide quadrangle of hardened earth and dry grass; along the south side ran the wall of the fort; ahead lay the sea. A couple of children found me on the beach, offering in their hands pieces of broken china, blue and white Chinese export porcelain. I found more shards washed up among the shells on a ridge of sand by the breakwater. Later a lone boy came with coins, Danish coins he said, though their lettering had worn smooth.

The entrance to the fort from the beach was blocked by a barrier of woven thorns so I went back and through the single gate that broke the wall along the parade ground. I climbed the ramp to the parapet and watched the sea in the heat until the waves seemed molten, then moved to the narrow shade of an embrasure above the gate. Opposite was the seashore bungalow. It was a lovely colonial building, arcaded all round. But it was falling into ruin: the sea encroached on one side while on the other creepers overran the garden and a dark tree shouldered up against the walls. I would have thought the house abandoned save that two figures sat deep in the shade on the lower veranda and a dog prowled by the gate.

Close by was a Hindu shrine with a well before it. A woman came out to the well, drew some water to fill a brass pitcher and carried it away on her head. I took a photograph of her in the empty square – the only picture I took there, and it failed to come out. I returned to Mayuram Junction at three on the same train that had brought me in the morning.

2

A yellow door wedged open in a blue wall. In the storeroom beyond
a bunch of green bananas was strung on a line. A second yellow door
lay open to the bedroom, where Tom's cot stood in the little whirl-
wind directly beneath the fan – although the house was rented for
the cool season we had the fans going day and night. A power cut,
stilling them, created a silence like a vacuum which the tinny cries
of birds outside seemed too distant to penetrate. Tom stirred in his
afternoon sleep but did not wake, and a fine dew of sweat massed in
the valleys beneath his eyes.

It was the headmaster who told us to hang the bananas. He would
observe our activities from his veranda opposite, invite himself in as
he crossed the threshold and instruct us on housekeeping with a
flutter of fingers above his proud belly – or rather, instruct me while
using my husband as intermediary; I was not addressed directly but
referred to by third-person pronouns.

'How much did she pay for these bananas? Ah, she should have
asked me. You must hang them, so, as they ripen.'

Going out, he paused on the veranda, his bare toes curling against
the grit on the stone floor.

'There is very much dust here. With every shoe that enters comes
more dust. She must arrange for some kind of mat to be placed
before the door. And do you not have chappals? You will be needing
chappals. You will wear them to go out and discard them within the
gate. But take care you do not leave your good leather shoes there;
these may be stolen in the blink of an eye; many of the residents
have experienced such daylight robbery. No, you will want chappals,
like mine. She will purchase some chappals also. They are most
inexpensive.'

There was a name-plate at his gate, I. Wilson Rajanayagam, Headmaster – but the occupation was obvious on sight of the man, with

his steely hair and moustache, and his manner of stooping and frown-ing as he spoke as if to fix a small boy in his sights. Above the doorway a framed reproduction of Leonardo's *Last Supper* announced at once his religion and his education. In retirement he lolled on his veranda in vest and lungi, the *Indian Express* spread across his stomach. To take the ten steps to our door he would fold the paper, place it neatly down beside his chair and slip on his blue plastic chappals. Acknowledged as the English-speaker of the compound (though his intonation was at times incomprehensibly Tamil) he was anxious to be of assistance. He said we Christians must help one another.

In India doors lie open and people live close. They crowd in on the newcomer. The population statistic that is known objectively beforehand, becomes palpable from the moment of arrival, even on Tranquebar's sketchy streets. At Tranquebar, people spilled up to the last lip of earth before the beach, where the fisherpeople had their huts. Right at the water's edge there were figures: men squatting to defecate before the wave line, others scrabbling for a living, panning for gold among the ruins by the fort, women and girls scooping the sand for mussels, or running into the waves to net the shells churned up and in by the sea.

One morning we drove the hundred and forty kilometres to Pondi-cherry and not for a moment was the road ahead clear of people. In the dust at the edge of the asphalt people walked. Or they padded single file along raised paths through the rice fields. People were not dwarfed by the landscape here as in the plains to the north. The land behind Tranquebar was delta land, flat, soft, green, every stretch of it bearing the imprint of man. Higher up the delta, irrigation works were being constructed on the banks of the Cauvery river almost two thousand years ago, under the early Chola kings. Men had cut the geometry of the wetland fields, dug the ditches and irrigation canals, built the dykes and threshing floors. They had planted coconut palms, bamboo and teak, and the palmyra palms that stood like chim-ney brushes along the canal banks. They had planted the rice that gleamed in the fields in December, whose green varied from one square to the next. (The youngest stalks were vivid as fresh lime leaves, standing reflected in the water with which the fields were flooded, the tone deepening as the plants grew denser and matured.)

At the Café Pondichéry on the promenade – self-consciously French like the public park with its low-fenced lawns and the white stucco streets that bore the names of Dumas, Romain Rolland and Suffren – I met a colonial British couple. The Mannings appeared so true to type that at first they were hard to believe: she, vague, with pretty white hair, wearing a blue-sprigged print dress and a necklace of coloured beads; he, bearded, wiry, brusque, jabbing the air with the stem of his pipe. In Britain the type is regarded sentimentally, as a picturesque anachronism. Here they were no more fossilised than the label on the Bhutan marmalade jar or the 1930s-style settee supplied to order at Spencer's Department Store in Madras. Pat Manning worked in import-export in Madras; Ursula found the heat more oppressive with age and now spent most of the year at Coonoor in the Nilgiri Hills. 'The house we have there belonged to a daughter of the old Maharaja of Cochin, you know. She had it as a summer villa.'

They met in Burma before the war, married just before the Japanese invasion and got out in the nick of time. When they first disembarked in India, Pat gave Ursula a morning in Bombay to buy all their furniture. Like our first day when my husband David went into Karikal, bought camp beds, bedding, table, chairs, steel cups and plates and cutlery before noon, and the cotton mattresses were made up and the whole lot brought twelve kilometres in a trailer on the back of a bicycle and delivered to our door by ten past three. Ursula gave a half-smile. 'So much stays the same here. Look at the bag that man's carrying, the little cotton shopping bag with the printed advertisement on the side. I remember noticing those in Bombay. The same. But then it's different too, isn't it, for you now? Different to be on the ground, so to speak.'

I asked if British India was crowded. Pat said it was, even then, but that it was a question of degree. 'The population increases at a rate of twelve million a year. That's practically the population of Australia added each year. That's a million a month. Think how many babies have been born since we started talking here. And that's just the net figure.'

Pondicherry offered relative spaciousness but at the library of the

École Française de l'Extrême Orient on rue Dumas the archaeologist Dr Françoise Léonore lit an untipped cigarette and shrugged as she observed that even in Pondy you noticed every year how there were more people as the press increased on the streets.

But Tom loved the crowds. At fourteen months, the world is spectacle, and India was more vivid than anything he had seen. At Madras airport we had been met and garlanded by a friend of a friend, a woman in a sari of scarlet and green. In the car to the hotel he had stood on the back seat and turned round and round to watch the traffic behind, in front, through every window, the mad weave of lorries, three-wheelers, bullock carts and bicycles. One night in Madras we saw some classical south Indian dance, a girl in gold-threaded silk and golden anklets. Tom escaped us and stood before her, mesmerised by her fingers and her feet and her eyes. The movement of the eyes was choreographed, a part of the dance, but hers kept returning to him as if she were dancing to him instead of to Krishna or whoever was the subject of the piece. When the dance ended, she came, a slight Tamil girl, and picked him up to kiss him, but he cried in horror as if the sun had come down from the sky.

We went to a temple. I wanted to say, look, Tom, look at the pyramids of red and yellow powder on the stalls before the gate, look how the elephant's face is painted. There was no need. His eyes had lit up already, his finger was pointing. At Chidambaram we ran into a temple festival. Through the packed streets surrounding the temple came huge wooden festival cars, wheels taller than a man's head, carved with multitudes of deities and covered with hoods of coloured cotton whose tassels swayed as a hundred men heaved at the ropes to pull them onwards. High on the cars sat impassive brahmin boys, and in the throng before them brahmin priests held aloft brass trays of burning camphor like waiters bringing flambé'd delicacies. Someone gave Tom a windmill of coloured paper. He took it grandly as a raja, riding on his father's shoulders, as later in the heart of the temple, he took from a priest a banana that had been given in offering to the god.

There were other things I did not want him to see: the obvious things, a leper, a beggarwoman's emaciated baby, the fly-stuck carcass of a dog. Few villagers had seen a white baby before. They reached to touch him. Some pinched his cheeks and then blew a kiss of praise on to their bunched fingers. Others reached too eagerly and their touch looked abrasive, though Tom seemed unaffected, too young to be self-conscious and without fear of the mob. In Tranquebar at first he drew a crowd, and even when we had been there some weeks I was to have the feeling that strangers saw him more as a pet or mascot than as a child. One day I was walking down the street with a friend and Tom was asleep on my shoulder. A woman I did not know tried to take him from me and he woke and cried. I complained to my companion and the woman apologised. She had children herself; she would not have been so clumsy with one of them; but she had not thought the little yellow-haired boy would wake, he was so like a doll. In India European babies grinned toothlessly on advertising hoardings and cans of powdered milk and cereal, Nestlé's cherubs, soft, fat, pink-and-white. Some people even pinned pictures of them to their walls.

3

A funeral procession came down King Street. Hindu funerals have
the glamour of festival, led by temple musicians with drumming and
trumpet blasts. The body was carried shoulder-high on a bier strung
with marigolds. Only men took part in the procession, a hundred or
more: Hindu women stay at home when their dead are taken. The
body on the bier was that of a young man, good looking, with a slight
dark beard.

King Street was far from the aquatint I had in my memory. It was
hardly ever empty, usually a flurry of villagers and bullock carts
before the Landgate, parted hastily at the hooting entrance of a taxi
or of the nuns' jeep. Yet it became possible to explain the desertion
of that day in June: in the hot weather the mission schools are closed,
not only St Theresa's training college but the girls' high school
attached to it, and also the Lutheran men's teacher training college
by the parade ground. Whoever remained in the village would have
been shut away indoors through the midday hours between the train's
arrival and its departure.

Our landlord Sheikh Allauddin lived on King Street in a Danish
town house with six Ionic columns at its entrance. He was a Muslim
and a rich man in the village. He owned perhaps the finest house and
certainly the one in best repair. He rented other property besides
the house where we were living, and he had a position in a shipping
office in the nearby town of Karikal, where he rode every morning
on a new red scooter. He must have been about forty, always fastidiously dressed in cream shirt and white dhoti, a little plump with ease.

When we visited we were offered the customary cup of sweet
milky coffee, sitting on metal chairs at a smeared metal table in the
hall. This was a long, tall room and there was no other furniture apart
from half a dozen similar chairs ranged along the walls.

Sheikh Allauddin let us first cool the coffee in the Indian way by

27

pouring it from steel cup to steel bowl; his conversation never pressed. He relaxed and waited until we had sipped.

'Your accommodation is satisfactory?'

'It's very new and very clean.'

'Good. For I do not wish to talk about that. I do not like to muddle business with pleasure.'

The formal courtesies were made informally. On the open stone floor Allauddin's son spun a wooden top, unleashing it like a weapon from its coiled string. Across the room stood a glass aquarium where Tom watched the circlings of colourless fish.

'I have a brother who is working in London. I wonder if you know the district . . .' He rose and went through a red curtain at the end of the room. Through the gap I glimpsed a desk awash in papers. When he came back he was carrying a pile of letters on a steel spike. One was from his brother, the printed letterhead that of a restaurant in East Ham. He had another brother who was working in Paris, where he himself had spent ten months.

'Paris was very fine. I was a young man, I was employed in a car factory and the pay was good. But one of us had to come back. Our family had this house. It was I who came back and it suits me here.'

The house had been part of the dowry of his mother, who had belonged to a prominent Tranquebar family. He showed us up a wide staircase to the roof above the second storey. It was a flat roof with a balustrade all round, higher than the neighbouring buildings, with a view across them and over the tops of trees to the echoing balustrade on the roof of St Theresa's convent above a glow of bougainvillea. In the centre was an airy upper room, narrow with long shuttered windows that opened to the sea breeze. At this time of year it was unused, stacked with wooden furniture for which the family appeared to have no need. To the back of the house, overlooking the garden, a bench was set into the white parapet.

I said it was a lovely place to sit.

He shrugged. 'It is cool.'

I asked if he knew that number six King Street had been built by a Dane called Muhldorff, who was also the architect of the Landgate.

Again, he shrugged. 'Some years back there was Danish engineer who came by the house and he told me the same. I believe it is true.'

Matthias Jurgen von Muhldorff was reputed to be an illegitimate son of King Frederick V of Denmark, exiled to Tranquebar for his part in some political conspiracy. He landed there in 1778 and remained until he died, aged eighty-six, in 1836. There was supposed to be an archway somewhere bearing the inscription 'DEMEP *anno* 1791'; in which, romantics claimed, lay a concealed clue to his royal identity.

Sheikh Allauddin looked down over his garden. A few mangoes, papaya and banana trees, a rubbish heap, a well and a tethered cow. Gardens that looked lush from outside, with trees spilling above their walls, were almost always disappointing within, the ground bare and dry.

'There was an arch here. Danish. In the course of some renovations we had to move it. We would of course have preferred to keep it in one piece but it was broken.'

His regret was mild. The house was where he lived. He saw no need to question its history. He became animated when he talked of business and of concrete things; of the building of the new mosque; of the shipping trade at Karikal and Nagapattinam; of local scandals. Chief among these was the problem of the village water tank, erected only in 1985 and cracked within four years because, it was said, after all the usual pay-offs the builders had had to skimp on materials; the pattern was being repeated as the municipality worked to gain state government clearance for the lakh or more of the rupees required for its repair. These, after all, were the things that mattered.

Later, in one of the cemeteries, picking a path through thorns, treading warily for fear of hidden snakes, I found the grave of one of Muhldorff's daughters, Maria Barbara Stevenson, and close by those of her two sons, Major E. B. Stevenson and Willoughby Carter Stevenson. On the hot stone of their tombs someone had placed cakes of cow dung to bake into cooking fuel.

Perhaps it was only the European eye which saw in Tranquebar a special place. Much of it was no more than a dusty shambles, indistinguishable from a thousand other south Indian villages.

If you came by bus, as most did since the railway line had been closed down, you got out on the main road at the undefined patch of earth they called the bus stand, past the Landgate and the moat. Beyond, the village overflowed on to the low-lying land by the river, where people made clearings in the thorn bushes and built huts of mud and palm-leaf. Along the road ran a line of shanty shops that extended into the market area. There, on the ground beside the shops, poor women squatted before pieces of sacking on which they displayed heaps of windfall nim berries or the dregs of the morning's catch of fish, bony silver fishes coated in sand. The women chewed pan with eroded teeth, looking nowhere, as their hands flicked at the flies. Poverty made grotesques of them as they aged, desiccating their bodies under scaly folds of skin until their breasts hung in neutered flaps that they left bare beneath the loose upper drape of their saris.

One morning I had my sandals restitched by the cobbler at the door of a hovel where his two small children worked in near-darkness winding lengths of thread. His wife made a crude attempt to charm me, offering a low stool and waving a palm-leaf fan at the flies on my face. Then she fetched out a collection of shoes from a heap in the corner, odd bruised court shoes, shoes with stiletto and platform heels, whose only use could have been to yield scraps of leather for patching villagers' sandals. I could not conceive what interest she thought they might hold for me. They made me think of the turning-out of dead women's cupboards. The cobbler charged me exorbitantly and I paid straight up, ashamed of my disgust.

Yet I found my reaction was rarely so simple. Often, the worst squalor is interwoven with beauty. Morning and evening a woman sweeps the dirt at her threshold and draws a kolam there, a traditional design, a geometric pattern or a stylised representation of a bird or animal. She swiftly marks the outline with a series of dots, then takes a pinch of chalk and links the dots with deft movements, sprinkling the powder evenly between thumb and forefinger. A girl buys an arm's length of jasmine for her hair but walks barefoot in mud. At times, these seem fine things. At others, they seem a gross reversal of priorities, and India's beauty becomes a mirage.

4

For more than two hundred years Tranquebar was the chief Danish settlement in Asia. It was where the first Protestant missionaries landed in India, off a Danish ship. And it was the birthplace of Catherine Noel Werlée, later Madame Grand, Madame Talleyrand and Princess of Benevento.

The Madame Grand connection is an irrelevant claim to fame. Her father was French, a port official by profession. Her parents' presence in Tranquebar at the time of her birth in 1762 was likely due to chance: the British had captured and sacked Pondicherry the previous year and many French had taken refuge in the neutral Danish port. Her mother was Portuguese or Eurasian, as it was to be whispered in Napoleonic Paris, though her portrait by Vigée-Le Brun records blue eyes and porcelain skin. Her voluptuousness, like that of Joséphine de Beauharnais, was to be attributed to her tropical origin.

She was first married at fourteen, in Calcutta, to Grand, an obscure if promising Swiss employed by the British East India Company, but a year later her life took a more dramatic course when the brilliant Philip Francis, one of the four members of Bengal's Supreme Council, climbed a bamboo ladder to her bedroom window. Francis was caught by the jemadar, challenged to a duel by Grand and eventually sued for trespass, paying up the huge and well-publicised sum of fifty thousand sicca rupees. Catherine left for Europe, to surface again in the Parisian *demi-monde* just before the Revolution. By 1797 she had set up home with Talleyrand, statesman and former Bishop of Autun. Her second marriage was reported to have been the result of Napoleon's personal intervention with the Vatican to release her lover from his vows. (The princely title was also Napoleon's gift.)

Tranquebar was then only one of many European colonies on the Coromandel coast. On seventeenth- and eighteenth-century maps, their names spill out one after another into the Bay of Bengal: Pulicat, Madras, Sadras, Pondicherry, Cuddalore, Porto Novo, Karikal, Nagapattinam, ports that were variously and at various times Portuguese, Dutch, British, French. The coast is flat, sandy, easily subsiding, and all the ports save Madras were open roadsteads, where ships must lie out as much as a mile beyond the groundswell and the offshore shoals. There was never much to commend them, never much to choose between them. And when the Europeans needed them no longer, their warehouses and factories were left like sandcastles before the sea.

At most of the minor settlements, little now remained. A fort still at Sadras, walls of narrow red bricks and within them goats and Dutch tombstones. Something like a classical temple on the beach at Karikal, a long bungalow with columns all round, perhaps a Customs house. At Porto Novo, only a fisherman casting his net into a grey lagoon, and four women walking into the water in their saris, wading to an island.

At Tranquebar the beach ran smoothly north–south as along the entire length of the Cauvery delta, sand unbroken by rocks. Only man-made structures disturbed its line. Beyond the open space of the parade ground, ruinous brick walls ran out into the waves, the remains of Danish or British breakwaters. Where these had failed, a round bite had been taken from the land. Colonial plans show whole streets that have been washed away just to the north. The last building now before the water was a fourteenth-century temple, itself half-demolished. To each side of it the land, which rose a metre or two above the level of the beach, had been cut back into small soft cliffs so that the only way to continue up the shore was to climb over the broken foundations and through the walls that once formed the enclosure. Waves beat against the rubble, breaking over fallen blocks of granite among the smashed brick, carved pillars, lintels and stalactite brackets of lost shrines. Flotsam collected there and men panned the wet sand for gold and coins.

A dwarf haunted this section of the beach and sold coins to occasional visitors. He was stubby and strong. Often he stood right at the end of the breakwater where the perspective exaggerated his height against the flat expanse of sea. He was educated and spoke fair English. He said that the old street of the goldsmiths had been submerged close to the temple, but he never had gold to show. Only blackened British coppers, one-quarter annas, Tamil coins, pea-sized roundels with curling lettering, and coins that he said were Danish but that bore the VOC monogram of the Dutch East India Company.

When we went to the beach we usually walked southwards, away from the temple and past the Danish fort. The fort had served for a period as a gaol, and that was what many of the villagers still called it. Its walls formed a quadrangle, long, low, irregularly notched by embrasures, prison grey from a nineteenth-century coating of concrete. The moat and the southern river entrance had disappeared long ago as the river silted up and shifted away. On the north the wall was broken by the main gate, a baroque archway in a faded yellow colour with shallow pilasters and a wide flat pediment. Goats browsed on the thin grass of the courtyard within and women came to the two wells to draw water. In a corner a broad ramp led up above the Danish factory storerooms to a platform facing out to sea. The upper storey had the same marzipan colour as the gate, its rooms a museum housing colonial relics and the jaw bone of a stray whale. Its architecture recalled Tanjore rather than Copenhagen, the work of Indian master masons lent to the Danes by the Nayak who ruled the district. A single sentry box remained on the north-east bastion, and one cannon pointing out to sea.

Between the fort and the sea lay matchstick ranks of beached catamarans. In the shade of the walls fishermen sat to mend their nets – white nylon nets, the gift of recent Danish government aid – which they stored beneath beehives of palm thatch at the end of the parade ground.

The fisherpeople were distinct from the rural Indians, a separate caste – in some parts of the coast, further divided into two castes of sea and river fishermen. At Tranquebar their huts clustered along the shore close to their beached catamarans, some by the fort, the majority behind the longer beach to the north of the village. The catamarans were primitive craft, made from three or five thick planks curving a little towards the prow, lashed together with coir rope and secured by a couple of concave wooden braces. The beams were so heavy that they could only be carried individually, so the catamarans must be dismantled on the strand each time they were brought ashore, with two men to take each beam up beyond the tide line. Going out, the crews reassembled them at the water's edge. It was a battle to cross the surf, two men with paddles, two with poles; the catamaran, with the leader standing at the bow, riding up to forty-five degrees at the crest of each wave. Sometimes a crew judged it just right, ran directly out beyond the surf, while others who started before them threshed in a trough between waves only a few yards from the shore.

Once at sea some of the catamarans raised a single mast carrying a triangular sail the colour of rust. They rarely went further than five or six kilometres out and on calm mornings a great fleet could be seen from the shore. The boats were so flat that the sails appeared to stand directly out of the water.

A cyclone passed, out in the Bay of Bengal. A day later we could still hear the surf from the house. On the way to the beach we met Indra.

'Beach?' The village had already observed how we went to the beach at the end of each afternoon.

'Beach. Come with us.'

Indra looked after the baby next door. She was Hindu, from a fishing family, and lived in a hut close to the Danish fort. She was fourteen and had left school a year previously with a collection of English words but without much grammar to link them together. Her wide white-toothed smile was beautiful in her long face and her loose limbs fell naturally into classical poses. It was rare to see her without the baby Sherbin on her hip, a solemn boy with a silver chain around his waist and a gold cross at his neck: his grandfather was the Lutheran pastor. Indra worked from six in the morning until evening every day of the week; for pay she received all her meals and forty rupees (about one pound) a month. Of this she regularly squandered a few paise on new plastic bangles and sellophane packets of ready-made bindhi – glued dots of red or green felt to decorate her forehead.

A gritty wind swept down the length of the beach. The tide had just begun to ebb, leaving a hard wet strand before the breakers. In the intervals between the waves, tiny crabs shot from their holes to scoot across the glossy surface and wild gusts sent some of them rolling like tumbleweed. We walked out to the sandbar where the old port had been. Behind it the rivermouth had swelled almost into a lagoon. Only a narrow channel cut through to the sea, and there three fishermen stood shoulder high in the surging water to lay nets. Indra took Tom and faced the sea, racing forward to dare the waves then pulling him back from the froth at his feet with a scream. The fishermen came out of the water. As they passed us they stared at the blond baby in the arms of the girl. They were naked save for roughly tied loincloths and turbans, small men with hard thin bodies, carved muscle under blackened skin.

Just south of the fort, a lone palmyra palm stood on the crest of the beach. Before the tree was a box-like shrine of whitewashed concrete no more than a metre high, its deity concealed behind a little wooden door that faced the sea. A metre in front again was set a Saivite trident with three yellow limes speared on its prongs. Some fifty metres directly inland, a second shrine stood among the thorn bushes, a flatter concrete box topped by a painted cone like a crude model temple.

As we walked back I asked Indra what god lived there.

She opened her eyes wide and shivered.

'She is a god of the fishermen. The sea is dangerous. She must not be angry.'

To keep her happy, each fishing family spent fifteen to twenty rupees for the annual puja, a ceremony of propitiation when in the middle of the night they sacrificed goats and cockerels before the shrine.

'She is greedy. They give her many things, cigarettes, brandy. Men drink much brandy that night.'

A palm appears in a similar position in an eighteenth-century plan of Tranquebar which itself is thought to be a copy of one from the time when the colony was founded.

Jon Olafsson, in Tranquebar in 1623, walked the beach as we did. He remarked on the silver of mica in the golden sand. He saw catamarans that differed from those of the twentieth century only in that their sails were made of woven palm leaf instead of canvas. He also saw larger boats that were made like Arab dhows from planks

35

stitched with coir rope and caulked with coir fibre. We found a boat like this, pulled up on the southern section of the shore close to the shrine, perhaps twenty foot long, with a three-masted yacht and a steamer painted in shades of blue on its prow.

Yet in one major respect the India he observed differed from that we saw. Olafsson was an Icelandic peasant who had bartered his first passage overseas in lengths of homespun and barrels of fish oil; in Iceland then, the unit of exchange was a dried codfish. At Tranquebar he met dealers of jewels, fine cottons and silks, and saw them trade in gold and copper coinage. Where he came from, they grew no fruit but summer berries, yet at Tranquebar there were two rice harvests a year and in the market he could buy mangoes, bananas, citrons, pomegranates, coconuts and sugar cane. India had stunned him with its wealth.

5

At the row of shops by the bus stand, a man kept bicycles for hire. He had a loose smile and his black hair wore an Elvis sheen. He looked as if he liked his work. In the morning he tinkered with his bikes and when they had gone, as they mostly had by half past nine, he leant on the rail between his shop and Paris Tailors, talking with the boys at their treadle sewing-machines beneath the roughly painted sign with the Eiffel Tower logo. At noon he took a chair over to the opposite side of the road to watch his shop from the shade.

We used to take his bikes, putting Tom in a seat on the handlebars, and ride inland. The original Danish possession was a strip of territory extending five miles along the coast and three miles deep. The coastal stretch was featureless: level sand and a retaining line of coconut palms or casuarinas, a few fishing villages that were more easily accessible by sea than by land, cut off by the thin waterways of the delta. The country immediately behind Tranquebar was mainly wetland, field after flat field of rice, but varied by the plantations of trees and the scattering of villages along the bends in the road.

There were small reminders of the Danish presence. A mile inland on the Mayuram road was a place people called the Mission Garden, the plot having been purchased by the Lutheran mission soon after it was founded in the eighteenth century. It was originally an industrial training home and it still belonged to the church, though it was now only a picnic spot. There was a pair of redundant gateposts at the entrance, a crumbling bench plastered to look like stone, and a path that curved and narrowed between tall mangoes and ran up to the dust clearing before the thatched hut of the watchman, to the well and the tethered cow. We went there often and the watchman's womenfolk nodded greetings, squatting on the step before the hut. The entire garden was overhung by the canopy of trees, the shade densest where the path split and wound through tight undergrowth, round small dark tanks where kingfishers surprised by their colour.

Not far off, up a dirt road at Sattangudi, was a second garden known variously as the Solomon Garden or the Brother Garden. This too had a remnant of a colonial gateway, and a section of wall with a baroque scroll at its end. Within, scores of goats browsed the thin pasture, on slightly undulating land that was raised a little above the surrounding rice-fields and planted with old mangoes, tamarinds and palmyra palms. For a brief period in the late eighteenth century a rival mission had set up a community at the Brother Garden, a party of Moravian Brethren bound for the Nicobars. They had landed at Tranquebar, unannounced and unwelcome, in 1760, to await there a ship that would take them on to the islands, which had been annexed by Denmark six years before. But no suitable ships appeared and it was another six years before the first of them could go on. At the Brother Garden they lived a communal and self-sufficient existence, though occasionally wrangling over Tamil souls with their fellow Christians down the road. The settlement continued even after the Moravians reached the Nicobars, but folded when that mission returned, defeated by the disease of the jungle islands. By the end of the century all the Moravians had returned to Europe; and in 1848, three years after the sale of Tranquebar itself, the Danes let the Nicobars pass to Britain.

At Tillially we looked for the country residence of a Danish governor. We had only a photograph to go by: a garden, a broken column and a flight of steps leading down to the river. We got no further than the temple in the village, where a thin young man asked us for a donation. It was a big temple, but run-down, its red brick almost stripped of plaster, its courtyard oddly like an English churchyard under the mossy shade of a huge mango.

'This temple is the temple of Sarandhaikathaswami. It is three hundred years old. It was built by King Vikaramachola of Tanjore. Its land amounts to nearly three hundred acres, wet and dry land both. It is now administered by the Hindu Religious Charitable Endowment Board. Ten per cent of revenues go to the government.'

We were speaking to the temple accountant. He took us to the pavilion which served as his office and sent a boy for coffee. His desk was close to the entrance, in the light. The dark behind smelt of bats. In a cell protected by iron bars stood an image of a bull.

'Silver plated. Made five hundred years back. Costing today five lakhs. We have highly – by that I mean extremely – costly objects in the possession of this temple.'

The accountant pulled out a printed paper pad from beneath a tower of curling files. His fingernails were painted with red nail varnish. 'I will give you a receipt for your donation. Name? Address? How much will you contribute to this temple?'

'Five rupees.'

'Five.' He made it sound mean – which it was – but he continued. 'Enough. This is enough.'

He stamped the donation form and receipt, asked me to sign. But he did not tear off the perforated section of the form. 'This I must forward to you by mail when all has been correctly entered.'

We asked if he knew anything about a Danish house at Tillially.

'Not at all. Of that I know nothing. But there is Gandhiji's monument, that you will see on the road as you go. Erected 1969 – no, 1949 – at the place where Gandhiji sat.'

'Was Gandhi here, at Tillially?'

'Yes, many years back. Nineteen-fifteen. There was a freedom fighter born in Tillially, a woman, Valliamai. She co-operated with Gandhiji in South Africa. For him she sacrificed her life, taking herself a bullet that was directed to his heart. She was an unmarried woman, only sixteen years old, the first woman freedom fighter in Tamil Nadu. Gandhiji you must know studied with one great pundit in Tamil. His name, Subramanian Achari.'

He had folded our five rupee note in his fingers. The donation form was left on the desk, the receipt never to be received in the weeks that followed. When at last we left, we saw Gandhi's monument, a crude cone of concrete topped with a budding lotus, painted in ice-cream colours. A chain with broken links symbolised the fight for freedom. A few blades of grass in the surrounding enclosure stood for a lawn.

By the river facing Porayar, we did find the ruins of a European villa. A Danish architectural survey called it the house of a Captain Smith or Schmidt. Only the foundations remained: the house had been set on the bank with the ground floor raised above steps at the front; the porch, looking down to the river, had had four columns. Across the river stood a modern shrine and a group of low village houses. A pair of banyans overhung the concrete ghat there. It would have been hot in the mornings on Smith's veranda. The sun glared straight ahead, the river was glassy and on the bend downstream palmyra palms reared against a metallic sky.

In the eighteenth century, sea captains of many European nationalities were based at Tranquebar. The Danish port offered a flag of convenience to the owners of private tramp ships in competition with the great Dutch and British monopolies – interlopers, they were called, the word deriving, not surprisingly, from the Dutch. Legitimately, they traded in cotton, indigo and slaves. Less so, some carried arms, profiting later on from the wars on the coast between the British and the French, and from the growing demand among Indian princes for European weaponry. Many, like Smith, must have become very rich. If they did not return home as nabobs, they could settle on country estates behind Tranquebar, plant mangoes or tamarinds instead of oaks.

In the National Gallery in London, beside the Gainsboroughs, I had found by chance a portrait of the British-born captain of a Danish East Indiaman. Joseph Greenway is set by the Danish painter with his back to a beech tree on an estate near Copenhagen. A hunting dog is at his side. His legs are loosely crossed in flesh-coloured breeches; his navy frock coat hangs open revealing a silver-buttoned waistcoat; in one hand he holds the hat just removed from his powdered hair, in the other a slim bone-topped stick. He has a well-made but fleshy figure, his face ruddy, his eyes blue and direct. The view over his right shoulder runs through a wood to the sea, where a three-masted ship lies before the horizon. Joseph Greenway was born in Devon. He amassed a fortune in the East India trade and was granted Danish citizenship in 1785. On his return home he became both Sheriff and Mayor of Exeter.

There was another house the Danish survey called McLloyd's. It belonged now to a Muslim, Thaiub Ali, and he called it Burke's

Garden. He knew nothing either of Burke or McLloyd. His father had bought the place forty or fifty years previously, when it had been wrecked by a cyclone.

At the entrance, on the Mayuram road, the old iron gates were pinned open by rampant bougainvillea. Only one section of the house was habitable, of two storeys, oddly bow-ended: Thaiub Ali said the design was his father's own invention, 'half-egg shape'. Around this, remnants of a classical building stood strangled in creeper: a pilaster supporting a strip of shattered architrave, a line of six arches that must once have opened on to a veranda and now formed a boundary to the back yard where chickens pecked beside the well. In front of the house was a large tank where coconut palms dived for their reflections among the lilies. At the centre of each of its four sides a flight of stone steps rose from the water between heavy balustrades, and at the base of the steps closest to the house a plastic soapdish lay ready for bathing. The family lived as much here, under the palm-thatch awning before the tank, as they did indoors.

Thaiub Ali was middle-aged, with a thick moustache and a broad wave of greying hair. His wife looked younger, with a long elegant face, restrained but rather fine like the single gold bracelets on her arms. Both of them had roots in south-east Asia as well as India. She had been born in Malaysia; his father had come to India from Indonesia in the 1920s. Photographs of Thaiub Ali's parents hung on the wall by the front door, and alongside them, one of Rajiv Gandhi. The parents were in black and white and solemn as deathmasks, the politician in colour, garlanded and smiling. Thaiub Ali was Tanjore District President of the Congress Party Minorities Cell. In a wallet he kept snapshots of himself greeting Rajiv, and of meetings with local Congress leaders.

He held himself like a man of position, seated upright on a bench that was set into the landing above the tank steps. His wife and two of their four daughters stood back a little way, and some distance behind them, a stocky youth – a Christian by the cross at his neck – who was their employee. Thaiub Ali had worked overseas, like many of the Muslim men in the district. For a few years he had lived in Dubai, where he had had a shop selling ayurvedic

medicines. But now there was only Burke's Garden to support
the family.

'There were thirteen acres when my father bought the orchard.
Today we have half that only. On my father's death the land was
divided between myself and my brother. My brother was not a good
manager. Recently he sold his portion of the land to a third party.
That was a wrong thing.'

His son was to tell me later that the two brothers were no longer
on speaking terms. The uncle was a wastrel, a mean man and a
jealous one who hated to see another get on; he resented Thaiub Ali
for his studies and for his politics.

What was left of the garden barely yielded the family a living. They
had five hundred small guava trees, twenty mangoes and two hundred
coconuts. They had had to fell a hundred coconuts the previous year
because there was no irrigation for them. The whole delta, and this
area in particular, was suffering from drought since the neighbouring
state of Karnataka had restricted the flow of water through the Mettur dam, higher up the Cauvery. Where they had formerly had two
acres of good paddy, yielding two crops a year worth five or six
thousand rupees, they would now be lucky to make one thousand or
fifteen hundred rupees.

'And I have a qualification in medicine. I can tell you that the leaves
and the fruit of the tree beside you – you call it the Indian fig – contain
twenty-one different vitamins and minerals. And the leaves of the
tree there, the sarakonai or drumstick tree, when pounded with
turmeric, make an ointment for bee stings. But what is this when I
cannot produce the dowries for my daughters? For each one, I must
have one or two lakhs. Two lakhs, for this Tanjore district is the
very worst. Here, the bridegroom's family will be asking that as
minimum, including scooter or car, furniture, servants and gold.
Dubai was a fine place. Watches, videos, calculators, all technology
is dirt cheap, and the Arab husbands pay to the father of their bride
five to ten lakhs. I think my daughters must marry Arabs.'

'Would they like to?'

'They complain, they would not like to wear the black dress of
Arab women. They are too vain.'

He laughed but the girls looked restless. One of them came and took Tom from my lap and skipped off with him across the yard. An iguana moved suddenly in the dark elbow of a tree and she raced round to see where it had gone.

The shade was green with the reflection off the water, the garden distractingly close. A hoopoe landed with open crest on the edge of the roof. A golden oriole darted like sunlight across the tank. Thaiub Ali said the oriole was 'a very eatable bird' and I saw that a catapult lay to hand on the balustrade.

6

In a village eight miles away I had met a man loafing in a temple. 'Are you Danish?' he asked. 'The Danish Prime Minister came to Tranquebar, ten years back. By helicopter he came.'

The Prime Minister's visit had gained the status of myth in the district. It had also had a practical outcome, in the ensuing grants of Danish aid for the fishing industry in the village and for the restoration of the Zion Church.

Built by the founders of the Danish colony, the Zion Church was initially attended exclusively by the Danish and European Protestant community, while native converts went to the New Jerusalem Church built by the Mission. Under British rule it became Anglican; after Independence, Church of South India, though as the congregation disappeared it became merged with the parish of Nagapattinam.

When I saw it first the building had been almost derelict. For restoration it had been gutted, doors and windows stripped out, pews pushed up against a wall. The vault over the nave was filled with criss-crossing wooden scaffolding for the plasterers. Heaps of plaster rubble lay in the churchyard between the cracked obelisks and squat areca palms. A few goats browsed there and a neat pile of steel cooking vessels stood beside the well. The sexton and his family – wife and handful of dark and smiling children – lived in a palm-thatched hut beneath the west wall of the church.

The sexton Isaak had heard that I was a writer.

'Papers, madam, we have papers.'

He dragged out from his hut an ancient trunk, opened it with a key from a jangling bundle.

'See, madam.'

The trunk released a dry smell of dust. Inside it were wads of letters, loose bills, faded registers of services and celebrants whose names were familiar from gravestones. The papers were brittle, disintegrating inwards from their margins. Their feel seemed to contain as much history as the information written in them.

I met the parish priest, Reverend Williams, in Nagapattinam.

'You are living at Tranquebar, at Tarangambadi?' He spoke of the village by its Tamil name; he himself was Tamil despite his English surname, adopted by his family as was common on conversion to Christianity. 'But what can you find to do there? It is enough for me to conduct a service once a month, perhaps to walk just across to the old gaol and to see the beach. The beach is very fine at Tarangambadi.'

He had come to the door of his presbytery surrounded by yapping Pomeranians, a big messy man with baggy cheeks and baggy cassock. He welcomed us, shooed away his dainty dogs and sent a boy out to buy a chilled mango juice for Tom. 'Isn't it hot for a little English boy?' The litter on his desk stirred as he turned the fan on to full speed. He caught a few flying papers and trapped them beneath a weight. I asked a couple of questions about the Zion Church and its restoration but he brushed them aside. That was all the Bishop's concern. The Zion Church was lucky since the Danish Prime Minister had visited it. What of other churches that were less fortunate?

'In Nagapattinam once we had a big congregation. Multitudinous. But this town is declining. Madras long ago took away the shipping. Nagapattinam is not a good port, you know, the ships must stop a mile from the shore: if there is one there today, you will see.' Not only had the British administrators gone, but also the visiting seamen who had come to the Protestant church, and even the Anglo-Indians. There had been a large mixed-race community descended from Portuguese, Dutch and British settlers, but this had shrunk since Independence. Most had left the country, discouraged from staying even by the railway which had been a major employer; they found work more easily in Australia. 'Now the Muslims are taking over the place. They have money. They work overseas, they make money there and they buy houses here. But they do not care for the town outside their doors, for the drains or the pavements. You see how it is crumbling.'

He unlocked his church. It was fine and solid, barrel vaulted, with dark stained woodwork, gallery, Corinthian columns, grandiose pulpit. He said it was founded by Danish missionaries. 'Did you not see the tablet on the wall where we entered?' We looked again. I told him that the inscription was Dutch, not Danish – after all it was the Dutch who had held Nagapattinam. 'So it is Dutch? Denmark is not Holland? What is Denmark, then?'

That afternoon I met Nagapattinam's Roman Catholic priest at the old Portuguese church. 'Have you seen the CSI church?' he asked. 'It is very well built. It was built by the British.' Europeans were interchangeable in this town, on this coast. As he put it, 'There were the Portuguese and then the Dutch, then the French drove the Dutch out and then you British drove out the French.'

And the British were long gone. A neoclassical Customs house looked out across the main harbour road and the railway line to empty yards and a locked passenger terminal. In the old administrative district, the law courts had adjourned for lunch. In the shade of a huge banyan before the driveway, clerks in white shirts and pressed trousers picnicked from tiffin cans. A modest circle of women typists ate their tiffin on the floor of an office upstairs, between the rows of heavy wooden desks with their black typewriters and papers weighted with stones. In the main courtroom, a picture of Gandhi hung crooked on the wall behind the judge's bench, and a wire mesh spanned the ceiling beneath the dome to keep out the sparrows that flew in through its glassless lantern.

The town had empty spaces – the gap between native and colonial centres, old and new towns, somehow never quite filled in India, left a no man's land as between Old and New Delhi. But land prices were beginning to rise with the opening of oil fields in the countryside along the coast. There was hope for the place.

Nagapattinam's last boom had been a crucial factor in Tranquebar's decline. In 1845 when the British acquired Tranquebar, the two ports were close rivals, but the British liked Nagapattinam and soon opened a railhead there which stole most of the regional trade. The Collector's Office was removed from Tranquebar, and in 1884 the District Court went to Nagapattinam. Only a Customs office remained and Tranquebar continued a thin foreign trade, which consisted by the early 1900s mainly of the export of paddy and of small numbers of coolies to Mauritius.

One of the last British-employed inspectors at the Customs house was Matthew Maguire's great-uncle, Tom Ballard. Matthew had told me his story.

'Tranquebar was not a family station in those days. Tom Ballard had been to one outpost after another. Maybe that was his trouble. He was of respectable stock, descended from a rubber planter in Penang who had married a Malay. The Ballards were rich; there was a Ballard Street in Perambur where we lived; and his father had been assistant station master at Cuddapah.

'Uncle Tom married a girl from Mangalore and had three children but he went the wrong road. He wandered off the straight and narrow. Took to drink, and worse. It was a sad thing since I have a memory of him before he fell into these traps, a handsome man riding a horse. Tranquebar was his last respectable posting. After that he took to the road and the railway, travelling the length and breadth of India and he never bought a ticket. There was some quality in him, he never lost it: though he'd come down to their level the rickshaw men and the coolies respected him. Every couple of years he'd appear at our front door. Uncle Tom Ballard. We'd take him in, give him a bed and feed him awhile and then he'd be off again. Sometimes he went to see his daughter Renée in the Carmelite convent. Or he went to Mangalore, stood in the street outside his wife's house but she wouldn't let him in. In the end though he died in her arms. He was taken ill somewhere up in the north, got straight on a train south all the way to Mangalore.

'The last I saw of him was in 1941. I was in the Wiltshires, at a barracks in Bangalore. He dropped by and asked for me, and the sergeant had him wait in the guardroom till I was found. By the time I got there he'd persuaded them to do a whip-round for him.'

Tom Ballard's Customs house, the Salt and Abkari Office, was one of the buildings facing the parade ground. It had been the residence of Danish governors, later the site of the District and Sessions Court. Since Independence it had fallen derelict and some time in the 1980s the Tamil Nadu Tourist Office provided it with a caretaker who slept by the door day and night. Little had been done to halt its ruin. From the ground-floor veranda a rickety wooden staircase, blocked by a barrier of woven thorn, led to a jalousied landing with doors opening on to the first-floor rooms. A smaller staircase inside must have led to the third-floor balcony, narrow beneath the overhang of the tiled roof. Looking back at the village from the beach, this house stood out from the rest, yellow, decaying, anonymously official, the shadowy upper storey rising clear above the palms.

JESUSWAMI

7

The Indian village sprawled over the area of the colonial town, so orderly in Danish engravings, laid out as it was on broad axes, enclosed behind glacis and hexagonal bastions. The most densely populated section now was the labyrinth of fisherpeople's huts north of the original line of the walls, while at the centre of the old town were places where the European street plan dissolved into path and thicket, and butterflies hovered in the light between the creepers and the thorn bushes.

We made morning walks to the shops by the bus stand or to the dhobi in the former Prince Christian's Street. The dhobi washed in the morning, ironed in the afternoons, using a great brass iron filled with hot coals. A short cut to his shop wound up an overgrown track to the gate of a temple (the gate half-hidden from view by bougainvillea, framing within its opening an inner gate and the doors to the shrine) then around the temple walls. In the mornings the streets were busiest. Few households owned a fridge so most people shopped a day at a time, carrying their small purchases home in white cotton bags. They greeted Tom with calls of 'thambi', little brother, and we would stop and any errand took a long time. Tom would make us stop again to look at the goats, the black kids with wooden tri-angles around their necks to curb their browsing, at the slow cows and the buffalo at his tether in the shade by the temple gate. Then we had to look at the pictures on the walls, the emblems of political parties stencilled on the side of every house at the last election: the orange hand of Congress I, the black and red sunrise and the striped flags of the DMK, the black and orange cockerel of the AIADMK who would have won Tom's vote.

It was on the second or the third day that we met the retired pastor A. S. Rajendram, calling good morning from his veranda at Flora Cottage just across from our compound gate. Rising slowly from his upright wooden chair and placing a steadying hand on the doorframe, he invited us in. Albert Samuel was his name, AS or ASR since the bishop had called him that at the time of his ordination. His father too had been a pastor, his grandfather a farmer, his great-grandfather the convert to Christianity. His late wife was the Flora after whom the house was named.

His servant brought coffee, a broad-faced girl with very dark Tamil skin that deepened in the glow of her burgundy sari. From a cupboard ASR brought out a red apple for Tom and polished it between his hands.

It was an old house, one of the few Indian-style houses in Tranquebar that had more than one storey, painted green outside and with an elaborate kolam drawn daily by the servant girl before the steps up to the veranda and the heavy wooden door. The room where we sat was whitewashed, with the usual line of metal chairs against the back wall. A low window with an iron grille looked on to the banana trees and the well in the courtyard. Beside the window was a cane-backed chair and a small wooden table with barleysugar legs; on its top lay letters, fountain pen and open spectacles.

'I first came to Tranquebar in 1952. It was later, but many years ago now, that my father-in-law made the downpayment on this cottage. I retired here in 1976 and now I am seventy-six. Tranquebar is a peaceful place. You leave the hubbub behind you when you enter the Danish gate. Do you know its Tamil name? Tarangambadi. That is the song of the waves. Tarangam means waves. So I live here to listen to the song of the waves.' He enjoyed making the English phrases.

His face was sensitive, deep shadowed. His body had thickened with age so that he moved deliberately as a turtle on sand. (The carcass of a giant turtle had been washed up on the beach after the storm, with scaly truncated limbs, vestigial fingers on its flippers, gaping mouth and opaline eyes.)

He said he lived simply on his pension of five hundred and twenty rupees a month; like other Indians speaking of money, he named the sum as a matter of fact, with no more emphasis than an Englishman might give to the statement that it was raining. His church defined his world. Of his four sons and three daughters, most worked in

Church organisations though one managed the YMCA in Madras; it went without saying that all had married Lutherans, save the last daughter who still lived at home and taught at the Lutheran school. Once, when he was a young priest, he had been sent abroad. He had visited the mission headquarters in Leipzig, and on the way home he had spent three days in London at the YMCA by Tottenham Court Road.

High on the wall was a photograph of himself and his wife taken just before he set off on his grand tour; his face was fatter then with a solidity befitting a Lutheran pastor. Beside it were other black and white photographs, of his marriage and of his father GSR in dog collar. A couple of religious pictures hung opposite and a print of a painting of Gandhi walking out from a village.

When he was not at his letter-writing at the table by the garden window, ASR used to sit by the front step and watch the street.

His veranda faced on to one of Tranquebar's grand houses, a dilapidated mansion in an eclectically colonial style, all balconies and colonnades. The house appeared to be falling into ruin though the date included in the plaster decoration of the parapet was no earlier than 1937. The view from the veranda revealed the extent of the ruin. You saw that the rooms of the upper floor had quite disappeared from behind the façade: there was no more than the balcony lunging from precarious metal brackets, and the gaping wall behind without its windows or doors, and beyond that the sky.

ASR said that when he first came to Tranquebar the Muslims who lived in the house were still rich. 'They were a big family with many sons. They worked here and there and they sat in the house and by and by the money ran out, the land ran out and they took out the doors and the windows and sold them. I have seen these carried away from the house one by one. Now they have nothing left to sell, except the house, and that they cannot sell. It is the whole family that owns the house, you see, and they are many and they cannot agree. So one of them lives on there and the house is ruined about him. This man has three wives, one Muslim, one Hindu, one other – though not all live there with him. The other men of the family I think are working overseas.'

That resident was an uncle of Sheikh Allauddin's. From Sheikh

Allauddin I discovered that his grandfather's will had contained a clause specifically preventing the sale of the house except by family consensus. Sheikh Allauddin said that the house was indeed being dismantled piece by piece, from the top downwards. There had been a fine domed room on the first floor with mirrored walls. Nothing of that was left. But if anyone were to have made an interesting offer, he believed that legal impediments might have been circumvented.

'He is my uncle,' said Sheikh Allauddin, 'but he is not a sincere man, not honest. Have you not seen him, a man in a Nehru cap?'

8

An epitaph in one of the cemeteries claimed a Magister Jacob Worm as the first Danish Apostle to India. Worm was a poet, satirist and pamphleteer who found himself deported to Tranquebar in 1681 and ended up as choirmaster at the Zion Church. There is no record of any conversion, no proof of his evangelism, only the epitaph and a story or two: that he performed miracles; that one day the sound of his preaching paralysed a Hindu procession, which could move on only when he fell silent.

A monument to Tranquebar's first accredited missionary stood on a corner of the parade ground, in the garden of the Lutheran teacher training college: a bust of a portly eighteenth-century figure set on a concrete pedestal with a green metal parasol over his wigged head. His name, Bartolomeus Ziegenbalg, was given on the plaque below. The parasol housed a single electric light bulb, illuminated every evening, and in December it was draped with a fiery string of Christmas lights that showed all the way down King Street. These went on just before night fell around six, and ten minutes later they would flicker and fail, like all the other lights in the village, for the brief duration of the evening power cut when, as it was explained, the local electricity supply was switched over to a second source. They did not regain their full brightness until after eight – the demand was so high during the intervening hours that a fan stirred no more air than an egg whisk and it took thirty minutes to boil a pan of rice on an electric ring.

I had imagined Ziegenbalg thinner, tight lipped. All accounts have him as a difficult character: zealous to an extreme, intolerant and bad tempered; this exacerbated by the terrible prickly heat he suffered in India and his refusal to leave off either his black wool overcoat or his periwig. He was voluble in his disgust at his fellow Europeans at Tranquebar and dismissed the majority of the natives as lazy and indifferent, reserving respect only for the brahmin pundits with whom he studied the Tamil language and discussed theology – and annoying his superiors in Europe by suggesting that Indian philosophy might actually surpass that of the Ancient Greeks. His work however was admirable – and more tangible than Worm's. He gave Tranquebar a church, a school and a seminary; translated the New Testament and the hymnal into Tamil; and wrote home copious letters which advertised the work of the Tranquebar Mission throughout the Protestant world, read in America by Cotton Mather and in England to the young John Wesley by his mother – Wesley would have been three when Ziegenbalg first set foot on the beach at Tranquebar in 1706.

The church he founded, now the Tamil Evangelical Lutheran Church (known always as TELC with the Indian habit of abbreviation, each letter pronounced with fast and clipped precision) had become a powerful organisation in Tamil Nadu. It worked independently of the European mother Church, though charitable funding still came from Germany and Sweden. It ran schools and institutions, orphanages, hostels and training centres, in most of the major towns. In southern India in particular, the educational system was heavily dependent on Christian foundations.

At Tranquebar, where there was no Hindu school, the TELC ran a boys' junior school. The buildings were in Admiral Street, centred on the Old Prayer Hall erected for Ziegenbalg's Mission. It was not far from our gate, the destination of morning crocodiles of boys – children of local Christian and Hindu families and from the nearby boys' home. In a parallel street, in another Danish building but one that was crumbling and condemned, the Church had a hostel for old men and in a complex of buildings on King Street, the Ziegenbalg Spiritual Centre continued active mission work. Bible readers went out to the villages, and Hindus came to its few bare rooms for instruction. The worker who managed the Centre, who was born of a family with a hundred-and-sixty-year history of Christianity, said that they made around three hundred converts a year.

Reverend Johnson was the pastor in charge of the Centre. He was a Tamil but married to a German, and they lived in a big house on the parade ground with a balcony facing the sea. Their walled garden flamed with different varieties of hibiscus and bougainvillea, red, purple and amber yellows. He was said to be a clever man but he held himself at a distance from the village; some believed that he was brilliant, others that he was cunning, or both. It was Reverend Thambiah of the New Jerusalem Church who was responsible for pastoral work. Johnson was the intellectual. He spoke European languages; he had lived many years in Germany and Sweden; he wrote; he discussed theology; he did not give to the poor, though his wife was loved for doing so, but he was considered to be incorruptible.

While TELC members no more than hinted at scandals within the Church, Muslims and others who observed them felt no such need for reticence. One pastor's daughter had recently gained a coveted teaching post at the school where he was governor. There was a rumour circulating that the TELC made a decision to suspend him in consequence, but that the plan was leaked a day in advance and the pastor had taken immediate sick leave, making his recovery only at the end of the suspension period. His daughter still had the job.

I wanted to meet Johnson but he seemed to evade me. I heard first that he was out of station. Then I was told that he had a fever. At last I met his wife in the street. She told me quietly that Johnson had typhoid; the mystery was to save alarming the village. I barely saw him all the time I was at Tranquebar.

His wife Eva Maria had pale skin and reddish hair and wore a sari quite naturally but looked big-boned beside the Tamils. When we met she often talked intensely. If we met in the street she would directly move into the shade so that we could speak in comfort. I noticed that most of the villagers who passed us would stop to make her a respectful namaskar, the Indian greeting of joined hands. She was known to everyone in the village and many of the boys had attended the school, of which she was principal.

She spoke with directness. She believed that the most practical thing Christianity could do for India was to teach people to be responsible for themselves and their actions: if you have only one life, she said, you take more care about what you do with it.

'Some few days ago a young man died here in King Street. You must have seen the funeral. His family are well-to-do. Nadars.' (The name was that of both a family and a caste.) 'They live in a fine old Danish house. Their relations are educated, with good jobs in Madras. But do you know what he died from? He had chickenpox. Chickenpox is the gift of the goddess Mariamman. The family would not call a doctor because to do so would incur the wrath of the goddess. He had some complication with the disease, a fever of the brain, and went into convulsions. Someone told the nun who is the nurse at the little hospital here; she came to the house and warned them but they did nothing . . . So, it is only one life. By and by, another will follow.'

This was shocking to her, the resignation of dharma. She found it impossible to accept what she said were the three beliefs fundamental to the accumulation of thought that was Hinduism: caste, transmigration of souls and rebirth.

'Think now what it is to an untouchable or a blind man to be told, as the Christian faith can tell him, you are beloved of God. Not that you are paying for a past life and must wait for the next. Think what it is here when a baby is born crippled and people say: that is how it goes, he will not walk in this life.'

For many of the first missionaries, caste was the most shocking aspect of Indian society – after extremes such as suttee, melodramatically described by one European traveller after another – yet it was one which their Church came reluctantly to accommodate.

Hindus were receptive to talk of other gods. There was nothing in Hinduism to forbid acceptance of Christ and of Christian ideas and even rituals. Its most restrictive aspect was the sense of caste and the rules of pollution associated with it, by which not only brahmins but people almost all the way down the social hierarchy were variously made unclean by contact with those below. So while the egalitarianism of the missionaries, their interest in people whose shadow might not even cross the gate of a brahmin temple, attracted many low-caste converts, their contact with these people repelled possible converts from higher castes.

It violated caste for missionaries to enter the house of an

untouchable and then pass on to other houses in a different part of the village. A convert could become unclean by contact with them and by joining in a congregation with converts of lower castes. As a result he or she might be excluded from Hindu society: this could mean being cut off from family and denied fire and water from the common well.

The missionaries countered by providing within the Christian community the social support which converts had lost in their villages, and as Europeans in a European colony they could offer additional compensations. But, as they trained catechists at the Tranquebar seminary, they found it necessary to set them to work exclusively with people of their own castes. Thus they began to conform with a system that went against the grain of their teaching. In time it became possible for converts to continue to observe caste after becoming Christians. In some churches separate services were conducted for high and low castes, and in others separate seating was arranged. The cruciform plan of the New Jerusalem Church at Tranquebar lent itself to convenient divisions of the congregation, male and female, high and low caste, along its three aisles, though Ziegenbalg, who had attempted to keep caste out of his religion, would have been enraged at the suggestion that he had planned it that way.

In the presbytery by the New Jerusalem Church, Reverend Thambiah kept a handful of photographs of late-nineteenth-century missionaries, German and Swedish priests and their families sent by the Leipzig Mission which had eventually replaced the Danish one. Mounted on broken card from old albums, mushroom-coloured with age, the photographs were predictably colonial: gatherings on verandas and watered lawns, white children posing with an Indian nurse in the shadows, formal groups where the Europeans always appear at the centre. The Europeans are composed before the camera, bearded men and women with centre partings and leg-of-mutton sleeves. The Indians, as in all such snaps, come out looking thin and afraid, an impression created partly perhaps by a genuine distrust of the camera but exaggerated by their scanty clothing and by the way the whites of their eyes stand out against sepia-dark skin. The lone group of Tamil pastors who pose for the photographer look ill-at-ease in dog collars and European linen jackets.

The modern pastor Thambiah was elegantly Indian, tall, dignified, usually dressed in a lungi. He looked even finer in his black cassock, high in the pulpit. The Tamil Church may have come of age the moment the Europeans departed, free at last to follow its nature. Thambiah made his pastoral rounds by bicycle, and I saw him often returning down King Street, wheeling back slowly to dismount by the step before his door. Or he would sit on the step dangling his grandson Sherbin, Indra's charge. He would weigh Tom in his hands and comment on the difference in their size and the few months in their age.

'So much meat you have in England. Can the boy eat rice? Here we have fish. Can he eat fish?'

I said that Tom could eat rice, fish, vegetables, dahls. Everything but the hot spices.

'Yes. I understand that in England you flavour the food only with vinegar.'

In the main room of the house a poster of the Matterhorn hung above the television set, his aged mother slept on a mat on the floor and chickens wandered in from the garden. The family's cow was tethered out there by an old tamarind. She lowered her head to charge at strangers. She was a fine beige cow but she had calved in November and they said that it had taken her oddly.

The Thambiahs were of a low caste. So was Johnson – it was said that those who adopted English surnames on conversion were most often those whose Tamil names revealed low-caste origin. So was the retired pastor, ASR. Though he was a Christian of the third generation, and the son of a pastor, he still called himself adidravida. The name is the Tamil one for untouchable.

ASR laughed when I asked him about caste.

'We have our theory on caste: that we are Christians, that all are equal and that we have no such difference. In practice of course it has never been so. The proof is all around you.'

The mass of the TELC membership came from the lower castes, and also a large proportion of the pastors. Education was widely available and the educated, pastors and teachers, could improve their

social status. But when it came to the arrangement of marriages –
and nearly all marriages were arranged – it was almost as automatic
to marry within the same caste as to marry within the Church. The
possibilities for upliftment – as the Indians termed it – were limited.

9

Christians occupied four houses out of six in the colony where we lived, a majority that was unmistakable on Sunday mornings when the air rang with American-accented hymns, cassettes which the headmaster Wilson received by mail order from Songspiration Inc., of Arkansas. Wilson was an evangelical Christian and did not attend any of the churches in the village. Instead, he went out after breakfast and took the bus to the Sunday market in Karikal.

Around dawn every morning of the week, Wilson went up on to the roof of his house to pray, like a Hindu, in the open air. With the example of Hindu puja all around them, the elaborate private worship of Hindu gods, many of the Indian Christians were monastic in their devotions. Wilson's wife, in her few free moments, between her schoolteaching and the preparation of the meals and the washing of the vessels, sat in a chair in the hall and read the thick family Bible. One day when Tom was unwell, she came to him and made the sign of the cross on his head and murmured a prayer. And when some friends from another town came to see them after a wedding, they knelt down together to pray. The sound drifted over at lunchtime, through their open windows and ours: Wilson leading with a slow and professional resonance, the others adding their alleluias.

Over one holiday, the second of their three sons came home on a visit. I met him watching a football game on the old parade ground. It was a local tournament, with six teams from the district, and it had drawn a crowd. Men and boys filled the band of shade beneath the fort, backs to the long wall, while a score of others sat in late morning sun on the battlements above. Before the arched gateway of the fort, fishermen held their usual place and picked through a mist of nylon nets. Other spectators had gathered across the pitch, on the ground beneath the huge Alexandrian laurel by the bungalow on the seashore, or among the glossy leaves on its branches.

Wilson's son was an electrical worker in Trichinopoly. He was, I guessed, in his late twenties, clean cut, with a trim moustache and wire-rimmed spectacles, seen more often in trousers than in Tamil lungi. He had an M.Phil. in Physics from the college at Porayar; he spoke good English, read *Newsweek* and listened to the BBC World Service. He was soon to be married – the marriage arranged by the usual criteria of caste, religion and education; the honeymoon to be spent, according to custom, in Kodaikanal, the major hill station in Tamil Nadu. The furthest he had travelled was Bombay, where he went once for a conference on atomic research.

At first sight, he seemed a typical modern young educated Indian. He blamed corruption for India's ills, and put somewhere second to that the divisiveness of caste. He believed that the churches, like the state, should enforce a system of reservation of appointments for low castes. ('Do not fear that the brahmins will suffer through this. The brahmins do well enough anyhow.' A Chinese whisper of anti-Semitism seemed to have crept in with his Christianity: 'You know that the brahmins are a west Asiatic race. They are migrants from the same part of the world as the Jews.')

Reservations were at the time a big issue in the north. Recent government measures in favour of the low castes had set off violent protests, a number of high-caste students even immolating themselves as they saw their prospects of study places and employment taken away. I asked Wilson's son if he saw any evidence of change here in the south, and in the Christian community in particular.

He thought about his answer, looking out across the threadbare football pitch. 'Perhaps the TELC and the Roman Catholics have been here too long. They have the habits of caste and corruption. How can they change?'

'You mean they're too Indian now?'

'Too Indian, yes, perhaps.' He shook his head in vague agreement, moving it from side to side in that Indian gesture which seems so equivocal to the Western eye.

Then his look took on energy. 'Do you know Billy Graham?' He spoke the name of the American evangelist as if it were a Tamil word, Biligraham. 'Do you love Jesus? When I pray to Jesus I pray not for myself, for my family, my people, but for the people of all the world.'

He spoke as if his side had just scored a winning goal.

Evangelical Christianity was booming in south India. Billy Graham's tours had drawn huge crowds and inspired Tamil imitators. The message had energy and freshness: it had an individualistic fervour which may have appealed in a culture shaped by Hinduism; but I wondered too whether a part of the attraction was its more contemporary flavour, American where the established missions were old colonial, European. There was an American ingenuousness in the way Wilson's son talked, a touch of the banality of modern world culture, as if he wore 'I love Jesus' on a badge.

At Wilson's house were stacks of evangelical pamphlets, Tamil and English. In the English-language ones at least, the religious message was propagated by managerial men in bush shirts and business suits. *Jesus Calls*, for example, featured a fleshy middle-aged evangelist called Brother Dhinakaran. Extracts printed from one of the Brother's sermons gave his life history: how he came from an educated but relatively impoverished family (father a teacher), gained a B.Sc. and went up to Madras; how he roamed the streets unemployed and friendless; how he came to put his faith in the Lord; and how a letter at once arrived from his father who had found him a position with the State Bank of India in his hometown. The facts do not appear to reflect a miracle, but an everyday story of an Indian bank clerk – and so one wonders if the father had influenced a former pupil to get his son the job, or done someone at the bank a favour in the normal way. Brother Dhinakaran cites as proof of God's continuing approval that he succeeded in working his way up to a position of importance back in Madras. The Lord has compassion towards man's soul, he preaches, towards man's problems and his sickness, but also towards his prosperity.

If much of the pamphlet seemed to be addressed to the smug middle class, Brother Dhinakaran's spiritual campaigns reached a wider audience. Letters to *Jesus Calls* testified to scores of miracles effected during a mass meeting in Jabalpur: the blind made to see, the crippled to walk, the chronically ill cured, many of them specifying a moment in his prayer when they felt something like an electric current pass through them and recognised the power of God. The writers ranged from a nurse and a veterinary surgeon to school-children and simple labourers. There was a grass-roots power to the evangelical movement, free from the hierarchy of robed priest as well as brahmin.

At Tranquebar a group of Pentecostal Christians held prayer meet-ings twice a week at an old house nearby. The form was very plain. They gathered in a long room entered between ochre columns. The men sat or knelt on the floor in front, the women behind with sari veils drawn over bowed heads. At a table someone read from the Bible, and the congregation gave to his words the total attention of the illiterate.

I had wondered at first if the force of the missions in the village was not dissipated by the various kinds of Christianity on offer. Why did a convert choose one denomination over another? Was it purely arbitrary, chance dictating which piece of charity work picked on him first? I had underestimated the Indian capacity for religion. And I had forgotten how in Hinduism differing gods and interpretations could coexist without contradiction.

The Roman Catholics had a longer history at Tranquebar than any of the other Christian denominations. There had been Goan Portuguese traders in the village, and native converts, before the first Danes arrived. An old Goan church, built in the seventeenth century against a stretch of the original town wall, lay within the compound of St Theresa's girls' high school, a classroom now with a blackboard hanging in the altar recess. The nuns of St Theresa's, however, had arrived only at the beginning of the twentieth century, buying up a series of empty Danish buildings at the top of King Street. These now contained the school and a teacher training college, plus a hostel and work centre for young destitute women. The convent had been established by a French missionary order. It had a dark anteroom where visitors waited beneath the eyes of St Joseph, and a parlour where they drank coffee from china cups and ate dry sponge cake. One venerable French nun remained, Sister Anne, tall and transparently pale among the Tamil sisters.

Once there had been bitter rivalry between Catholic and Protestant missionaries. Accounts of the early Danish Mission include a strange report that a German traveller came to them having met a European blacked up and dressed as a brahmin somewhere near Cochin on the Malabar Coast. When questioned, the pretended brahmin had admitted that he was a Catholic priest, one of twelve to be sent undercover, by order of the Pope, 'to root out the Protestant faith in Tranquebar'.

The Catholics no longer actively proselytised. At the Portuguese church in Nagapattinam the priest had described how Hindus came to his Christmas crib. They made their ritual gestures before the baby Jesus in the manger, beginning with a gesture of humility, bowing the head and crossing the hands by the side of the cheeks, which he interpreted as having a meaning similar to a Catholic crossing himself as he enters the confessional: bless me, I am a sinner, or I am low and ignorant. 'The Hindus are very generous. They allow Jesus to be one of their gods. But they can do so and remain Hindus. Try to convert them and they come easily but they go easily.'

For those who had stayed Christian, there might be a variety of reasons. Negatively, there was some escape from the predetermination of caste, the practical enticements of charitable support and education, and those of identification first with the colonial ruler and later with the rich countries of the West. Christianity also offered an omnipotent god, so powerful, if they really believed in him, that he could overrule any number of local evil spirits.

The Mother Superior at the convent was a firm and clear-headed talker. Her looks had the anonymity shared by all the Tamil nuns: small figure, round dark face in the white habit. Hinduism, she said, was a religion of fear. The motivation of the simple Hindu, the village Hindu, was plain fear that if a man did not do as his father or his grandfather once did, his god would punish him. Shiva the destroyer was more potent than the preserver Vishnu.

We were walking back after Mass one Sunday. The Catholic church stood a half mile outside the town gate at Sattangudi, almost opposite the cinema. The returning congregation made a pretty procession down the straight road, with convent girls in long green skirts and hair tied with orange ribbons. The morning sun fell hot on our heads and the Mother Superior held her black umbrella for me to share.

She admitted that fear could be found in Catholicism. Fear of hell had been a driving force for many in the medieval Church – feudal Christians not so different perhaps from her simple Hindus. But the Catholicism she knew in India expressed immediate and positive sentiments. 'The Hindu comes to us because he sees our actions, believes in love, justice, charity. The things beyond that, ideas of heaven and hell, theology, do not play great part.'

So they did not preach. They concentrated instead on their charitable work and hoped by that to draw converts. In their school, when Catholic children studied catechism, Hindus had non-religious moral instruction. Many of these chose to convert after they graduated. Other converts came from outside, and she said that even when they had not come through the school, the majority were women.

'Is that because you are women?'

'No, I do not think so. The women come because it is always the women who turn first to religion; their men are too involved in the world.'

Even when none of the school was present, more than two thirds of the congregation at Mass were female. It was easy to estimate as the congregation was segregated, the men in the west transept behind the children's choir, the women packing the transept opposite and the main aisle with a stained-glass dazzle of synthetic saris, some on pews, some on the stone floor, often overflowing to the door where they left their chappals on the step.

10

A few days before Christmas, Ziegenbalg's fairy lights went out for good as the TELC college closed for the holiday. Tranquebar was emptied of its schoolchildren and students, and the Christian presence suddenly diminished. Even so this was still out of proportion to its number. A recent census of the population within the line of the old town walls counted a hundred and thirty-seven Protestants and a hundred and fifty Roman Catholics, beside five-hundred-odd Muslims and nearly a thousand Hindus. Perhaps the Christians felt a need to assert their identity more strongly.

Outside every Christian house hung a cardboard star, rigged up with an electric light bulb inside and shining over the front door. Star was the first word Tom learnt in India and soon the neighbours' children had learnt it from him. 'Star!' they cried as he pointed at one overhead, and skipped up to flick it so that the pinpoint pattern of light swayed across the ground and the walls.

We did our Christmas shopping at Karikal. People at Tranquebar said you could get everything in Karikal. The town had remained a French colony until 1954 and it was now Pondicherry Union Territory. The average wage in Pondy Territory was eight times that in Tamil Nadu.

The state boundary was a broken concrete bridge. (Weight restriction in force: if you went by bus, you stopped before the bridge and all male and standing passengers got down and walked across to rejoin the bus on the other side. The bridge had begun to go some years before and the routine had become automatic to all but the most important men in the district, men in white dhotis whose caste or position seemed to permit them to stay put, even to spread themselves more broadly across the seats so that there always appeared to be more people standing after the river than before.)

Above the muddy ribbon of water stood a police checkpoint, a barrier and a one-room bungalow with palmleaf matting over the windows. There was a restriction on the passage of liquor between the states, from the shops of liberal Pondicherry to dry Tamil Nadu. The open doorway of the bungalow allowed a glimpse of the official in control of the checkpoint, a fat man slumped day after day on a wooden chair, tilting it so that his feet rested on his bare desk. He wore reflecting sunglasses and his paunch bulged through his tight uniform shirt. He knew the local drivers and a look and a stiff nod were enough to stop them and pass them through, to save everyone the trouble of raising and lowering the barrier.

In Karikal, the roads were free of potholes and the drains worked. The town possessed two sets of traffic lights, each reinforced by a traffic policeman in white uniform and red gendarme's hat. There were STD telephones and private cars on the streets. Even the madman who ranted on the road past the bus station was modern enough to hold an imaginary microphone. The French had left behind some neoclassical public buildings and the large Roman Catholic church beside the boys' school. They had intermarried with Indians and every now and then a French face or figure stood out from the crowd on the streets. A nameplate read Jean-Luc Lejeune; beside the door stood a white-haired man with Gallic creases down his cheeks, gold cross dangling against his vest front. A girl on a bicycle had a thick black plait down her back; when we passed I saw that her features were Vietnamese.

There was a Vietnamese and Chinese restaurant and the shops sold Western foods: unsweetened bread, butter, tins of processed cheese, porridge oats, Nescafé, Rose's lime juice and bottled Pondicherry mineral water. In an arcade beside the mosque, Muslim shopkeepers displayed imported china crockery, glasses and enamelled metal plates, alarm clocks, toys and trinkets made in south-east Asia. They called this the foreign market. Quality here was immaterial; foreign provenance was all. The Taiwanese china cups bore shaky rosebuds, factory rejects, and the stainless steel teaspoons were bent. Muslims, more cosmopolitan than the rest, were the main customers. Village Hindus generally stuck to the purity of unbreakable Indian metal vessels. Everything was disposable, everything cheap, despite the importer's profit. I bought Tom an

Indonesian-made plastic jeep. I didn't expect it to last him more than a week. The shopkeeper said there was no market for anything good, anything that cost more than a few rupees. Even in Karikal few could afford it.

Our driver, Natarajan, came from the taxi company in Karikal (only the nuns and the Johnsons had cars at Tranquebar). He came for us once or twice a week, always twenty minutes later than ordered but reliably so. He had barely a word of English and I think he could not use a map: when we tried to direct him according to one he brushed the folded paper aside. Yet he found his way up dirt tracks to obscure temples, with the minimum of questioning of villagers through his rolled-down window – militarily brusque, the address of mechanised urban Indian to peasant. And he cared for his ageing Ambassador car by not driving it too fast. He was a big, dark, ungainly man with hoarfrost stubble and bloodshot eyes. He smoked untipped Gold Leaf cigarettes and had a wide, hoarse laugh. When we stopped in towns he would pick Tom up with his big hands and lift him shoulder-high to show him the crowds.

We drove from Karikal to Kumbakonam. The road ran straight and true to the state boundary then wound the rest of the way on a precarious river embankment. To one side lay rice fields. White egrets picked through the green stalks and brahminy kites wheeled in the sky. On the other side was the drop to the river, a delta branch of the Cauvery that was near empty, starved of water from the Mettur dam. It still held moisture enough for strip plantations of teak and bamboo thickets.

Natarajan wove round the bends and through the villages. People sat at the edge of the road before palm-thatched mud huts that were neat as if the clay of their walls had just been smoothed by the palm of the maker's hand. At the car's approach boys and grandmothers scattered like game, back into their tamped-earth yards. Only the ambling goats ignored us and Natarajan had to swerve for these. Or occasionally a daredevil boy would stand ground before jumping aside, or throw a stone. Then Natarajan would stop and bawl him out, to drive on with a shake of the head as if to ask, how do you teach these young lads a lesson?

Along the road were shrines to local gods, altars striped white and rust-red beneath old banyans, miniature temple structures, stiff concrete horses; even a concrete aeroplane had offerings before it. In each village was a temple and close by the tank for bathing, overgrown so that only the patch of water at the foot of the flight of steps was clear of lily or hyacinth. Often a village also had a political post bearing DMK flags and slogans. At one place a red banner was stretched across the road and we passed a Communist out pamphleteering, red scarf over one shoulder, hammer and sickle flag on his bicycle handlebars.

When we reached Kumbakonam Tom was asleep on my lap. David went shopping and I stayed in the car where the air did not move, rolling down windows of darkened glass. Natarajan leant on the bonnet to smoke a cigarette. Men cycled by carrying steel tiffin cans. Sunlight bounced off the silver metal but it soaked into everything else, held in the ubiquitous coating of dust. David came back with nothing more rare than two pairs of chappals, to satisfy Wilson, and a star for our door.

Kumbakonam was a famous brahmin centre but at first you saw only the improvised streets, the loose spread of the modern south Indian town. The temples were hidden and when you found them they were sad. Their paint-caked halls and gateways rambled outwards, like the town itself, from the Chola sculptures at their heart. In one temple courtyard heaps of rice lay for winnowing on a dirty pavement. At the gate of another a squadron of cockroaches scuttled by the step where we left our shoes.

The finest of them, Darasuram, lay in a dirt-track suburb. It was a complete architectural piece, a great Chola temple of the twelfth century. It was open and almost empty, clean sharp-carved granite. Striped squirrels skimmed across its hot walls and floors, and the stone was the same pale tawny colour as their fur. The brahmin guide looked a wild ascetic, long-bearded and ash-smeared, but spoke elegant English. He had a polished delivery for Western tourists. He drew biblical parallels to Hindu stories illustrated in the carvings on the walls, one to the parting of the Red Sea, one to Christ's miracle of the water and the wine, though the teetotal Hindu saint transformed his water to oil; and he compared the archaic smile of his

Parvati to that of the Mona Lisa. The smooth paving burned underfoot as he talked on. The handful of tourists shifted their weight from
one tender bare sole to another.

When the Chola temples were built, Tamil Nadu itself was the
home of an empire. Tamil Cholas ruled Ceylon, the Maldives and the
Andamans, fought campaigns in India as far north as the Ganges,
and overseas in what is now Sumatra and the Malay peninsula. For
centuries before that, the Coromandel coast had dominated the trade
of the Bay of Bengal, even that to China. It takes a full shift in
perspective to see the coast itself as the centre, when in later history
it has been viewed as peripheral – a place of transit for the Arab
traders who superseded the Tamils (the name they gave it, Ma'abar,
meant no more than that), and a halfway-house for Europeans.

On Christmas night the church choir sang carols before each starred
doorway in the village. In the morning we gave Tom his jeep and a
one-rupee paper kite. Wilson's cassette player bombarded the colony
with schmaltzy carols.

Wilson came to us with sparklers and firecrackers and a tray of
Indian sweets. Standing solemnly on the threshold, holding the tray
in one hand like a communion plate, he pronounced a blessing. 'May
the Lord, on this great day, bless these good people. May the Lord,
on this the anniversary of His birth, bless this family which has come
from afar.'

The cry of a beggar, 'Ma, ma!' from the gate behind him forced his
voice up to a volume that would have carried across five classrooms.
Tranquebar had only a handful of regular beggars but Christmas
brought a flood of professionals from outside: cripples with their
history printed in Tamil and English on a well-thumbed card, children,
old people, mendicant Hindus in orange rags. A beggar need not be
a Christian to stand beneath the star at a Christian home and offer
the householder a chance to gain a few paise's worth of karma (or
grace) by giving.

Weeks before, Reverend Thambiah had claimed us for his congregation by extracting from David a generous donation towards Christmas decorations. The New Jerusalem Church was festooned with
chains of yellow daisies and by the pulpit a casuarina stood in for a

Christmas tree. The main service had been held late on Christmas Eve. It was moving: Thambiah's voice coming rich and sonorous from the pulpit, the dark air weighted with the scent of the garlands in women's hair and of the frangipani tree in the churchyard, the veiled heads gently bowed over joined hands. The light Indian manner renewed the familiar European words and gestures. But I could not help seeing a mimicry in it. They sang 'Silent Night', beautifully, in Tamil, and they had never seen snow. Like perfectly schooled children, the missionaries' dusky lambs.

The celebration I glimpsed in the gutted interior of the Zion Church on Christmas morning owed little to Europe. The sexton Isaak, his family from the thatched hut, and a few others sat cross-legged in a cleared circle among the plaster heaps and scaffolding, chanting as a man beat out a rhythm on a tin. They were intent, the circle closed. I walked on.

At three I went down to the beach. When I turned the corner from Queen Street the gate to the mansion of Sheikh Allauddin's uncle stood open. He was there, the Muslim in the Nehru cap, stretched on a planter's chair in the recesses of the veranda, a lazy patriarch supervising from a distance the loading of a cart.

The sea was turquoise. The sails of three catamarans stood out like shark's fins, black against it.

Perhaps a hybrid culture was in the nature of this coast, of any coast but of this one in particular, jutting into the Indian Ocean between the paths of the monsoons. Tamils took Hindu ideas and architecture east from here across the Bay of Bengal – the great temples of Angkor Wat in Cambodia and Borobudur in Java follow a style born at Mahabalipuram on the Coromandel shore. Arab traders came from the west and brought Islam. Christianity had come to the coast certainly before the Arabs and possibly before the first Chola kingdom. There was a legend that the Apostle Thomas died at Mylapore near Madras. He was said to have landed in India in AD 56, on the western or Malabar coast, in the modern state of Kerala, which has a strong and uninterrupted Christian tradition. He made converts and moved on, setting up crosses and performing miracles. One of the miracles ascribed to him, told of Mylapore and of other sites, is typically Indian in its imagery, devoid of function: that while bathing in a tank he threw some water into the air and that the droplets hung there and were transformed into flowers. But at Mylapore St Thomas refused to worship before an image of Kali and was speared to death by brahmins.

His tomb there, tended by a small community of Nestorian Christians, became a great pilgrimage centre, visited in the Middle Ages by Marco Polo and other European travellers, then declining, to be revived and Catholicised by the Portuguese. It is recorded in the Anglo-Saxon Chronicles that in 883 a monk named Sighelmus, later Bishop of Sherborne, was sent from England by King Alfred in search of St Thomas's tomb and brought back precious spices and jewels.

11

It was the Portuguese who founded the pilgrimage at Vailankanni, just south of Nagapattinam. In the sixteenth century a Luso-Indian buttermilk boy had a vision of the Virgin Mary on the shore there and a shrine was founded where Portuguese sailors came to pray for safety. A hundred years later a Portuguese ship miraculously sailed out a great storm and the crew erected a chapel in gratitude.

The chapel was now a basilica, just a stroll from the beach. After three hundred years, Vailankanni had interpreted Portuguese pilgrimage in a peculiarly Indian fashion. It had also preserved a hint of British resort. On hotel balconies, names sprouted like bed-and-breakfast boards in Bournemouth: Little Flowers Shrine Lodge, Rosary Lodge, Villa Marya. In them I thought I could recognise the setting of Matthew Maguire's childhood holidays, the genteel Anglo-Indian pilgrimage of the 1930s.

But Vailankanni had grown brash since then, and it greeted all comers with frenzied commercialism. From the car park before the basilica, right to the sea's edge, the streets were filled with fried fish and ice-cream stands, and stalls selling the paraphernalia of seaside pilgrimage – an extraordinary combination of the sacred and the profane, rosaries, sunglasses, seashell mementoes, religious medallions, beach balls and pingpong bats. Beggars were as inevitable as the hawkers, and pilgrims were systematically harried from the moment they arrived. Women, children, legless and blind men, old men and orange-robed sadhus, worked between the ranks of cars and buses, then along the railed queues where their prey were trapped as they bought the obligatory tickets and candles. Business was so good that they had set up their own stalls offering small change. Neat towers of coins were lined up on a tabletop: nine ten-paise coins for one rupee, giving the banker a ten-paise commission. David changed a two-rupee note and was cheated, receiving in return seventeen instead of eighteen coins.

The basilica had recently been rebuilt on a huge scale – the number of pilgrims, like all the other numbers in India, having multiplied since Independence. The new church gleamed from the porch steps to the crosses on its spires and pinnacles, like tufts of white candyfloss against a postcard sky. Tall gates kept it free as Disneyland from the squalid hustle in the square before them, reserving the space within for a spectacle of efficient devotions. The pilgrims filed up the aisle and, with many genuflections and touchings of heads to the altar rail, before the golden-robed doll of Our Lady of Health. The image was set in the tiled reredos of the original Portuguese chapel which had been swallowed up by the new basilica and whose old rococo opulence was almost modest by contrast. Prayers must be brief for the press forced the pilgrims on to the left, where they planted their candles on iron spikes – and these were removed as fast as they appeared, pulled off in casual handfuls by the man who stood behind the rails, extinguished on a piece of sacking and thrown, still only fractionally burnt, into a tin trough.

In the Lower Church at the far end of the basilica, Mass was in progress. Sightseers milled amongst the pious who knelt on the marble floor. Over the altar a crucifix hung suspended in a frame of lights against a cerulean curtain threaded with Lurex. Beside Christ's nailed and outflung left hand, the Christmas star shot out above a huge plastic globe: inside the globe was a crib, revealed through the letters LOVE which were cut out and outlined in fairy lights. At the end of all this a staircase bore an enigmatic sign above its locked gate, 'The Entrance to Christian Life.'

The new complex had been constructed in the 1970s. A brass tablet on the wall of the Lower Church recorded the names of the parish priest of the day, the architects and the contractors, Mr Xavier Tamby & Sons and A. S. G. Lourdusamy Pillai & Sons respectively, Catholic firms by the name of the first at least, of Trichinopoly. Every man involved in planning and financing the project seemed to be credited somewhere, for temporal or higher good, even the Revenue Divisional Officer who had commissioned the motor pump room (Entrance Strictly Prohibited).

From the church, pilgrims walked the Holy Way to Our Lady's Tank, following a straight path between green watered verges, past brilliantly whitewashed and life-size Stations of the Cross. A sign reassured that All Buying and Selling was Prohibited, though a boy with an ice-cream box on the back of his bicycle dangled a melting cone through a gap in the high fence of woven barbed wire. Behind the fence spread a ribbon development of pilgrim hostels, charities and associated industries, from a Mother Teresa home to the surgeries of ayurvedic physicians advertising patent remedies: Oil for Bone Fracture; P. Thangavelnaddar, est. 1949, Bon. [bona fide?] Physician.

There was a shrine at the walk's end, at the spot where the Virgin had made her appearance, and by it the entrance to the tank where her supplicants queued once more to bathe in the holy waters. Everything here had been rebuilt too, the shrine a round concrete pavilion containing a gaudy tableau of the miracle, the golden Virgin sweeping down from the heavens to save a crew of muscular and moustachioed sailors, fairground figures who bared their chests in terror before a zigzag of lightning. All around, young trees gave shade for picnicking. Contemporaneous with the pavilion, the Shrine Cool Drinks Stand (Annai Canteen Branch) sold biscuits and orangeade.

A family from Pudukottai spread their tiffin on the ground. Like many of the other visitors, they were urban and middle class. The father wore jeans, his son Adidas T-shirt and trainers.

'Ah, Vailankanni is a wonderful place for a day out. Very modern. And my mother has not been too well of late.'

They came for the cure and the holiday, both.

'And then also, my son is preparing to sit examinations.'

The Museum of Offerings was packed tighter than the basilica. People shuffled single file along the railings before the glass cases where the silver gifts to the Virgin were displayed, exclaiming at one dedication after the next. Most common were tiny silver cradles, self-explanatory. A pair of silver crutches two inches high were the gift of the parents of a polio victim who had learned to walk. Only a small proportion of the dedications were written in English.

Thanksgiving to Our Lady of Vailankanni for all the favours granted to me. Bless me and my family. With Your grace I passed the MBBS and am now a doctor. Bless me in the upliftment of my career. As a token of my reward I keep this silver stethoscope at Your humble feet.

Dr (Miss) Bhanumathi Jayaraman, MBBS, Calcutta

Thanks to Our Blessed Mother for helping my husband and myself to build our upstairs building before my husband's retirement. I thank you my Blessed Mother for fullfilling our disier [sic] with your help.

Your loving children,

Robert and Mary Fernandez and family

At the Tonsure Hall which stood the other side of the taxi park, supplicants had their heads shaved before visiting the shrine. This building too was new, square and municipally brown-tiled. Close to the entrance, a tactless pedlar brandished a dozen black hair pieces strung from a pole. He stopped a middle-aged woman with a thin bun, took out a box of matches, lit one to singe the tip of a pony tail. Smell that, see it crinkle. That's real human hair.

Tickets were sold at the booth just inside the door: tonsure two rupees, ear-boring one rupee. Inside was a single room and all around the walls, boys and men sat on the floor to have their heads swiftly and functionally shorn. Some of the children cried and the sound reverberated off bare concrete. Among them a couple of sweepers worked lackadaisically at the growing piles of black hair, crouched over twig brooms like senile apprentices.

Women had their heads shaved in greater privacy on the upper floor. I spoke with one who came in, a small woman, girlishly frail. She had short grey hair and wore a homemade frock of shiny white fabric like a First Communion dress. She was accompanied by a friend, who wore a cotton skirt and blouse and a gold cross at her neck, her dark hair carefully curled to shoulder-length and not for sacrifice. They were Anglo-Indian and had made the pilgrimage from Calcutta, four days on a train, each of the last three years.

The woman in white spoke tentatively, as if afraid to crush her

78

meaning with coarse words. 'Four years back I was troubled with pains, terrible pains in the head. They said to me that I must have an operation on the brain. But I said, look at me, I am fifty-seven, I am a working woman; I cannot have this operation. Instead I came here, and since then I have been in good health. Thanks to Our Blessed Lady.

'In 1951 I had a tumour on my ankle. I said then to Our Lady, I will wear a white dress from this day on if I am cured. And I have. And the tumour disappeared. Can you understand this? Are you a Christian?'

I said that I had been brought up a Catholic.

She reached out her hands to me. 'Then I am glad to have met you. It is good that you are here, but it would be best for you to come in August. August twenty-ninth is the feast of Our Lady of Health. If you come then you will see the great work Our Blessed Lady is doing here. On that day they bring out the holy statue from the basilica, and each year two doves appear and fly above Our Lady's car, the festival car.' Her hands danced above her head. 'No one knows from where they come. And in September, when the car goes back to the garage, they go. No one knows where they go to.'

Two doves were said to fly like that over the festival car of some Hindu god. Many of the details of the pilgrimage were shared with Hindu myth and rites, like the tonsures, anointed with sandal paste, and the sacred immersion in the tank.

The religious cross-pollination has worked both ways. Hindus come alongside the Catholics to Vailankanni and take home pictures of Our Lady of Health to put up beside Shiva and Ganesh. They make a magpie selection from the images of Christianity – or chiefly those of Roman Catholicism, which has the best pictures. There is the Madonna, a gentle addition to the Hindu pantheon. She might perhaps be equated with the smiling Lakshmi, goddess of wealth and good fortune, though one could hardly imagine Lakshmi, pink and cur-vaceous and seated on her lotus flower, as a virgin. There is the Sacred Heart, hanging beside Ganesh on the sooty wall of the Tran-quebar dhobi's hut, back-lit, Pre-Raphaelite in its colours, at once gory and sentimental; and Christ the King, with crown, orb and sceptre in an advertisement for a popular ayurvedic toilet soap: Jesus saves your soul from sins, Medimix saves your skin from diseases. Then there is the Christ child, for whom there is no substitute among innumerable Hindu gods – an omission that seems surprising given the Indian love of babies, their fondness for posters of fat boys with kohled eyes and kiss curls.

The son of the brahmin priest at Tranquebar attended the Lutheran primary school there until the age of twelve. He was a bright pupil and was taken up by the Johnsons, often going to their house to read *A Hundred Bible Stories* and other things. One day Eva Maria asked him about the family's morning routine.

'We rise,' said the boy, 'then we have silent meditation, then we say a prayer.'

'And who do you pray to?'

'Jesuswami.'

When he was fifteen he let his hair grow into a priestly topknot and went to work at a temple.

12

In the great mosque at Nagore I stood in another pilgrim crowd, crushed beside a Hindu woman in a mob before a Muslim holy man as he blessed miraculous limes and threw them into the air above our heads. I'd been told that the limes gave a woman fertility but this woman was old. Perhaps they had other gynaecological powers. When she caught one she gave it to me, along with a handful of rose petals she wanted me to eat. She was a graceful woman in a bronze sari that matched her flecked eyes. She signalled to me to pray, raising her palms towards the sky.

There seemed to be always a festival somewhere. Often, as you stood at the bus stand at Tranquebar, craning to identify an approaching bus, you would see the word 'tourist' posted at the front in place of the destination, and the waiting villagers would shrink back from the road, and the bus would career by like an express train with a blur of garlands and a wake of dust. They'd say it was a pilgrim bus heading for some shrine or festival. For many Indians, pilgrimage was the only form of tourism.

The festival at Nagore commemorated the Muslim saint who brought Islam to the Coromandel coast and converted the local raja by a miracle. The town was predominantly Muslim, a plain south Indian coastal town, a grid of streets between road and sea, few of the buildings taller than the coconut palms. The mosque lay at the heart of the town, raising five stumpy white minarets above the low skyline. The surrounding streets did pilgrim trade, lined with shops that sold small luxuries, trinkets and toys, scarves and embroidered skullcaps, and dates, sweets and fruit that could not be found elsewhere.

For the twelve days of the festival the town was flooded with people. The crowd before the mosque was so great that its entrance, down a narrow arcade, was controlled like a lock gate by policemen and arm-banded Muslim officials. Hundreds of pilgrims camped inside, in the peripheral courtyards, beneath makeshift roofs of palmleaf matting. Each family there had a plot marked out with spread lengths of cotton, like bathers on a packed beach, where they whiled away the day sleeping with cloths over their heads, sitting cross-legged in tight groups, their few possessions beside them in cotton bags or shopping baskets of perforated plastic.

The atmosphere was different from that at Vailankanni, more ancient, perhaps, and the festival had drawn a high proportion of poor country people. The hustling seemed more pious, in the hall before the tomb of the saint, a place like a white-tiled crypt where sound and incense hung between the thick columns and beneath the low-vaulted roof. Men in white crocheted skullcaps peddled joss sticks and holy tokens of beaten silver. They sat in groups and waved pilgrims towards them with expressive fingers. One fastened upon us, an old man with a grey fringe of beard; pinned to his loose white shirt he wore a rosette like a political canvasser, the emerald green of Islam. He blessed us with a hasty flourish of incense over our heads. 'On this day whatever you wish will be given to you.' His outstretched hand closed silently on our donation.

The saint was buried in a marble tomb encased in beaten silver. Only men might approach it, so while David and Tom disappeared through silver doors I must stay back among the women before the heavily policed gate, as they murmured and chanted, those at the front clutching like prisoners the green-painted iron bars that offered a glimpse through to the lesser tombs of descendants of the saint.

Outside, over the open courtyard at the centre of the mosque, monsoon cloud loomed pewter above the tomb's silver dome. A wind stirred the pennant flags that hung between the minarets, which streamed out, long, forked, white marked with green sabres. People clustered around a pretty domed pavilion, where the holy man they called the Pir Sahib fasted in honour of the festival.

He was a fat man in a thick white turban, sitting cross-legged on a square dais. The pavilion was roped off from the crowd, and period-ically he was hidden from view as acolytes unfurled canvas curtains strung from the pillars on each side. There was nothing ascetic in his appearance. He was sleek, with smooth olive skin, lightly bearded,

like a plump sultan on his cushion. He stroked the folds of the voluminous cotton robe that swathed his body. He fiddled with the strings
of beads and garlands around his neck and ran his hands through the
piles of red and green two and five rupee banknotes on his lap, sifting
them among pink rose petals, limes and knotted cords like black
shoelaces. He did not raise his eyes to look at the spectators who
pressed towards him.

His acolytes fussed and circled round, clever-looking men and
boys, most of the men in dashingly wound green turbans. They called
out, took money from the crowd as if they were taking bets across
the ropes at a wrestling match. The punters jostled for position, but
good-naturedly, edging towards the arches of the pavilion directly
before and to right and left of the Pir. Suddenly, without any warning,
he would throw a lime out into the crowd and men and women would
scrum to catch it and the luck it would bring. They stumbled and
laughed and bodies pressed carelessly together. Those who failed
could pay two rupees fifty and receive a lime and a handful of rose
petals from one of the acolytes who themselves stuffed petals into
their mouths and munched as they passed behind the ropes.

As one surge in the crowd subsided, a bright youth landed up
beside us: 'Madam, that lime that you have will give you whatever
improvement in your life you wish.'

The festival was nearing its close, when the Pir was to be carried
out from the mosque to the seashore. There the boys and men would
race against him. 'You think he is fat but he can run faster than any.
On the seashore he will run so that none can catch him.'

But we did not get to the shore. The rain came, a downpour that
soaked the moment it touched, driving everyone under cover. The
Pir's departure was delayed, the acolytes drawing into a huddle
around their master. We waited at the edge of the white-tiled hall of
the mosque. Every inch of space was filled but the atmosphere was
quieter than before. The festival and the hustling were over. Beside
us a family sat in a circle, a young woman with a sleeping child in her
lap, an older woman praying with head raised, eyes half-closed, white
beads in cupped palms, mouthing a chant and rocking hypnotically.
The rain did not let up, but at last the Pir moved, carried on a
palanquin, preceded through the halls and courts by the jungle calls

of Indian trumpets and by drums and explosions of firecrackers.

He passed. We stepped out into the rain, ankle-deep in water, and others were swept forward with us. The Pir entered the passage that led out from the mosque. The crowd bottlenecked. When we did at last reach the gate there was nothing to see but the rain and the brown torrents that were the streets. We stood and watched among the people pressed under the overhang of the mosque roof. The water rushed by. A man waded across holding a black umbrella, stepping daintily in double-folded dhoti. A policeman with a military moustache ushered an important old Muslim into a waiting car, respectfully oblivious of the water that poured down his shoulders as he held his umbrella over the bent, skullcapped head.

13

The rain came again in the night and early the next morning. When it cleared, colours strengthened. Walls of ochre and turquoise, bougainvillea, palm leaves vitreous green, the sea's blue intensifying to that of copper sulphate. Mica glistened on the beach. Reverend Thambiah had been sitting on his doorstep as we passed down King Street. 'When the sea is soft,' he said, 'the fishing is good.' All day the catamarans were out on the water. A few carried sails, triangles of deepest maroon. The rest drifted. In the distance the low rafts and the raised arms of men with paddles were like torn branches on a flood.

The full moon rose early, so bright that when the sun went down inland behind the fort it already made a white track across the sea. Late that night, Queen Street looked clean and empty as in archive photographs from fifty years before, when the population was smaller and the colonial buildings were still maintained. The moonlight superimposed black-and-white order over its decay, hid the staining and erosion of stucco and gave crisp outline to buildings as to the arching leaves of palms overhead. Falling obliquely, it altered perspective, making the parade ground huge, the fort long and low. On the wooden veranda of the old Customs house lay shrouded sleeping figures. Beneath the lone lamp on the corner by the post office – though its light was barely necessary – sat a ring of fishermen interminably checking and mending their nets.

New Year's Day was another full-blown tropical day and the Christian girls came out in their best saris to go to church. In their hair they pinned garlands of marigolds or pink rose petals or some mauve trumpets they called December flowers. They giggled and called greetings as they passed. New Year was as big a festival as Christmas, and like Christmas it brought a stream of beggars to the gate.

A fisherwoman also came to us with a basket of fresh king prawns. We had long been looking for these. Bay of Bengal prawns were a delicacy overseas and the entire local catch usually went for export, swallowed up by the Danish-given freezer plant as soon as it was brought ashore. We had asked at the market and even at the offices of the freezer company; and at last, word had got through. The woman squatted on the doorstep to clean the prawns and Wilson's daughter Miriam made a masala paste, grinding a dozen tiny red cloves of garlic with peppercorns, cumin, ginger and other spices, rolling a cylindrical piece of granite up and down along a slightly concave block and moistening with water as she went. (A smooth and effortless process, it seems, until you pick up the stone and feel its weight. As in so much of the work of Indian women, the fluid movement only conceals the strength involved, the rhythm itself integral to the muscular effort.)

I stopped by the convent and witnessed the ceremonious New Year's greeting that took place between the employees – drivers, watchmen, kitchen helps, and labourers from the nun's small farm – and their mistress. The Mother Superior sat on a wooden chair, flanked by Sister Nirmala and another senior nun, and the men filed in. They wore long white dhotis and looked as stiff in them as European peasants in Sunday best. Each shuffled up with a gift of fruit, a lime or some bananas, or more extravagantly, a tray of oranges, grapes and apples (the last invariably bruised and woolly but considered a delicacy since they came from the cool of the hills). The workers knelt to be blessed, then retreated to join a shy semicircle around the walls. The Mother Superior made a brief speech in return and, taking from Sister Nirmala a tray of boiled sweets frosted in sugar, offered them around, at the same time pressing a five rupee note into each worker's hand.

I asked her later if she thought it strange for these men to be taking orders from women. 'Not at all,' she replied with a smile, 'they do what we say and dominate when they get home.'

And did the convent employ their families, their sons?

'No. There is no such job security.' She corrected me briskly. The ceremony was not to be considered so feudal as it might appear.

*   *   *

Sister Nirmala had found a girl to help look after Tom when David returned to England. She listed admirable qualifications: a Catholic girl, from a good family in the village, twenty-one years old, a graduate from senior high school who was waiting for a place at the teacher training college. She brought her round a few days later. Her name was Regina Mary and I liked her.

Wilson saw them going and stopped them for a quick word at the gate. His verdict was instant. 'She will be very good for you. Her father is Conductor, Cholan Roadways Corporation, Retired.'

He took the opportunity to check our own plans, addressing David as usual.

'And when will you be returning to Madras to take your wife home?'

'I won't be coming back. It's very expensive to fly from London to Madras.'

'So your wife will go alone? Is this conventional in England?'

'It's actually a very straightforward journey.'

Wilson swallowed disapproval. 'Well, I am sure you will be missing your family. In particular, your son.'

The morning David was to leave, taking the train to Madras from Mayuram, Wilson came to the door early.

'What time did you ask your driver to come?'

We thought we had allowed Natarajan time enough to drive to Mayuram, plus his usual twenty minutes' grace.

'Ah. You should have told him to come an hour earlier. These people are always late. You do not know. He will go somewhere else first, then he will stop to see his friends. You cannot trust these people. Drivers, servants, they are not what they were. They are always thinking they can be earning better somewhere else. What is the time now?'

'Still two minutes to nine. He's not late yet.'

'And then there is the traffic. I think you have not made the necessary allowance for the traffic. This is most unpredictable nowadays, with so many buses, special buses, taxis going this way and that.'

Wilson was at heart a Victorian, with his fine head of grey hair and full but trim moustache: upright, patriarchal, meticulous almost to the point of neurosis. He asked the time again every three minutes until Natarajan turned up, a mere fifteen minutes late. Wilson intercepted him before he reached our gate and gave him a dressing down that must have taken him back to his school days, and so impressed him with a sense of urgency that we were nearly killed on the road and arrived at Mayuram with forty minutes to spare.

When I returned later Wilson must go through each detail again. A journey was an important event, not to be taken lightly. 'In India it is most essential to arrive well ahead of time. One hour is often necessary. There is the requirement of buying the platform tickets, of ascertaining the carriage number and the position on the platform, the arrangement of the baggage and the hiring of porters.'

Only when a telegram came from London two days later was his mind put at rest. Uncertainties could be put aside. Arrival had been confirmed.

The same day that David left, the funeral took place in Tranquebar of a native evangelist who had died in America. He was born in a house on Admiral Street but he had left Tranquebar forty years before, to teach and evangelise in Ethiopia, finally going on to New York where his son worked as a doctor. He had returned to Tranquebar only at intervals of five years or more. Now his body came back air freight, to be buried in the family grave in the New Cemetery by the Landgate.

Though few people in Tranquebar could have known him well he was a significant figure for the Lutheran community. The funeral was attended by a solemn representation of the bourgeoisie, pastors, masters and their college-educated children. The dead man had been in some way related to the Thambiahs, and Reverend Thambiah officiated. His cousin was headmaster of the TELC teacher training college so eighty youths marched behind the coffin, dressed in white with black mourning tags on their shirt pockets – when you thought of it, half of TELC must be related somehow, with the size of families and the way marriages were arranged. The procession went past the family home and made a circuit of the village before entering the cemetery. As it came down Admiral Street, I saw that Sheikh

Allauddin's uncle slunk at its fringe, looking sinister and very Muslim among the TELC worthies; I wondered what he was doing there.

Next day a goat was nibbling at the wreaths on the new grave, head stuck through the freshly painted railings. Rev. Dr Massillan Daniel, born 30/11/1918, died 24/12/1990. I read the names of other members of the family: they included a Nathaniel, an Isaac and two Moseses.

VILLAGERS

14

My ironing cost three rupees. I gave the dhobi a five rupee note. Apologetically, he brought out a yellowed and crumpled two rupee note from a tin, then lifted the iron to press it before handing it over.

Life was made up of details. Regina Mary came in the mornings and I would write, explore, carry out the errands that filled the day. Often I stopped at the bakery by the bus stand (though bakery was too grand a name for a stall selling the sweet and insubstantial Indian packaged bread, stale iced cakes and biscuits). The boy there always had something to give to Tom.

'Where is your son?' he asked once.

'At home, sleeping.'

'Your son is very soft.'

And Thambiah had said that the sea was soft. The Tamil word was *menmae*: soft or fine.

There were new ways of doing things. Tom took his bath the same way as a child we watched being washed by the well. The boy stood naked save for a string tied round his waist. His mother drew up a bucket of water then squatted before him, her eyes level with his. She filled a jug from the bucket and poured water down his back and shoulders. She could be careless if it spilled on her sari since the sun would dry it. The actions were simple, with a closeness that is lost across the hard edge of a bath. There was the game of the water, the apprehension as the jug was lifted, the shock when it was poured, the rapid washing down from head to foot, then the repetition as a jug of clean water was lifted for rinsing.

I no longer found the house too close or too coloured. In the hall I had my table up before the window, with a view through the curling iron grille to the veranda, through a second grille into the light of the passageway and across to the mirroring apartment opposite, veranda grille, veranda and window.

The colony at sixteen Queen Street was barely completed. For the first few weeks a pile of rubble lay before the gate to the compound while a man and a woman interminably sorted the stones and broken bricks and chipped them into regularly sized hard core, and a baby Tom's age played in the chippings. The building was a home investment for the French earnings of Sheikh Allauddin's brother, new beside the decay of the street like a crisp franc note against a bundle of torn rupees.

Modernity was the unifying factor in its design, which seemed to have been made up as it went along. The street face was asymmetrical, one section painted with horizontal stripes, rust and white, the opposite one faced in shiny tiles the colour of dried oxblood, taller since it contained the stairwell to the flat roof. Between these lay the entrance to the passage that separated the apartments, bridged at the front only, and topped with a flimsy balustrade in colonial pastiche. Even when it was my home I found it no more personal than a cinema front, the grilled window to the left of the entrance beckoning me to buy tickets.

The passage was dirt, tamped and hardened by the passing of feet. Sunlight and rain fell only at its centre, in a narrow shaft between the overhanging sections of roof. Though the apartments had been occupied only since November, the two at the end had a few herbs already established along their walls, and some kind of cactus, said to deter snakes, had been planted at intervals between the individual gates. Two vipers had been killed in the garden during the rains.

Each apartment had two fair-sized rooms with ceiling fans, a third, airless room at the back with a single tiny window, a small dark kitchen, a washroom and a latrine. The kitchen was purely for cooking. Built in was a concrete counter and sink for draining, at low level since the Indian cook squats to work, and a concrete hood over the counter to draw stove smoke to the ventilation hole in the outside wall. Most of the food preparation, the chopping and grinding and the cleaning of fish, was done outside in the small yard at the back. There also the vessels were washed (vessels a term that covered pans and dishes, somehow more appropriate since all these were of steel or aluminium). Against the yard wall was a concrete water trough without a water supply. The pipe that gaped above it was neither fitted with a tap nor connected to any external plumbing; each morning the trough must be carefully plugged with a bung of cotton rags wound round a piece of wood, and filled with sweet water from pitchers brought from outside. The pump in the middle of the yard drew only salty water for washing down the tiled floors and flushing the latrine.

At first our pump had to be primed continually. David asked Wilson where he could buy a washer to repair it. 'No, no,' came the shocked reply, 'you will not do that. A skilful person can make it work. We have such people here. They are called plumbers.' A plumber was found. A small advance payment persuaded him to come within a day. He tinkered and somehow mended, and cost almost nothing. In India a man's labour is usually cheaper than any manufactured part.

The two larger rooms each had a fluorescent tube on one wall, a glass-shaded light bulb on the other; the smaller rooms had one light only. All the switches were grouped on the wall with the single electric socket. Each door had bolts inside and out, with fixings for a padlock: a measure against the pilfering that went on in the village.

When I told people where I lived they would look impressed and ask how much rent I paid. The new colony on Queen Street was said to be the best accommodation for rent in Tranquebar, the only one with indoor latrines and all facilities. It was almost as well equipped as the Johnsons'.

The neighbours were middle class. There was Wilson the retired headmaster, with his nameplate and *Last Supper* print at the door. With him lived his wife and one son and daughter; his two other sons came occasionally to visit. Next to him and directly opposite our gate lived a young man who drove a new red Enfield motorcycle. He was manager of a tea shop by the bus stand in Porayar, a modern tea shop with coloured bamboo awnings and loudspeakers. He was from a Porayar family and when his wife had their first baby early in December they went to spend the customary first six weeks with his parents so that the mother-in-law could supervise the care of the boy-child. On their veranda hung a photograph of a boat in the sunset with the words 'Oh God, you are so great and our boat is so small';

they were TELC. Beyond them was a Muslim household; above the door a piece of Islamic calligraphy reversed out from a painted mirror. A woman and two children lived a shadowy existence there while the husband worked in Madras. On one side of us lived Reverend Thambiah's daughter Shanti, the schoolteacher, with her school-teacher husband and the baby Sherbin. They too had a Christian seascape on the veranda. On the other side was a second Muslim family, three generations of women and girls dependent on the earnings of one man who was away in Singapore.

Few of them owned much furniture, or anything else for that matter. Even the teachers had scarcely a book in view. Their apartments seemed empty, furnished with perhaps a table, a token chair that was brought out when I came to visit, and bamboo mats that were rolled up when not in use. In most, the one substantial piece of furniture was the bed, a great marital bed of iron or brass or a solid platform of teak. Only Wilson's rooms were more crowded, with tables and chests, shelves piled with papers and beachcombed shells, and a goldfish aquarium. They planned to move it all to a larger house they owned in another part of the state when his wife also retired from teaching.

For myself I had a formica table, two upright chairs, a low cane armchair and a folding bed with a cotton mattress, the steel-framed type that was coming to replace the old string bed. The armchair I considered my one indulgence. The water that was brought in from the standpipe each morning was stored in two tall plastic pitchers in the cool of the passage leading to the yard, water for immediate use in a bucket in the washroom, water for drinking in a covered stainless steel vessel in the kitchen: all standard arrangements except that I then put the drinking water through a filter and boiled, bottled and chilled it. I was the only one in the colony to possess a fridge. I also cooked on electricity, using a single hob that we had gone all the way to Pondicherry to buy. (My demand for electricity was excessive: the circuit could not bear simultaneous use of fans, lights, fridge and hob.) The neighbours cooked on kerosene, wood and cow dung, all of which were more reliable considering the erratic supply of power. A gas cooker was a theoretical alternative but a licence was required for its use. In Madras the licence application was said to take three months but in Tranquebar Wilson had so far waited one and a half years.

The garden at the end of the passage was mainly bare earth, the surface drying back to dust soon after rain. There were half a dozen coconut palms between which the washing lines stretched, and a couple of nim trees with yellow fruits like crabapples, from which people made a medicinal oil. Wilson had made a thorn fence around a narrow strip adjoining his wall, and planted the ground with pink roses and scarlet hibiscus and other flowering shrubs. Though he had moved in only a few months before, a pumpkin plant already rambled over the fence and covered yards of the communal garden with its broad leaves and limp yellow trumpet flowers. At the end of the garden was the rubbish heap, which Wilson set a match to every week or so, but there was little rubbish save vegetable scraps and fish bones. Most goods came packaged only in newspaper wound around in cotton thread; plastic bags, bottles and airtight tins were kept and reused, or could be resold at the market. Whatever was left that could be scavenged was quickly taken by the crows or by the goats and stray dogs that wandered through the gate or across the tumbledown boundary wall.

To one side was the house of Sheikh Allauddin's uncle, to the other a vacant site, a plantation of coconuts mixed with flowering trees, the ground grazed by goats and tethered cattle. The smell of the livestock thickened the air that came through the little window in my kitchen. Sometimes I saw a white-haired man in the garden there, and often in the mornings a limp woman in a brown and orange sari. Men came to tend the trees, dark men, rakish in the uniform of their profession: rough-tied turban, loincloth (usually green), and heavy leather belt over the hips from which hung a hard pouch made from a gourd and containing knives with short curved blades. I saw one climb a tree just a yard from the window. High up, he cut a branch and let it fall, then threw down the axe. He unwound the red cloth from his head and knotted it in a loop, which he suspended from one ankle. Starting to climb down, he dropped his other foot through the loop, and using his two bound feet like a clamp on the narrow trunk, shimmed to the ground.

*   *   *

97

Over the walls at the back came the chatter that went with cooking and washing, but other domestic sounds were channelled down the passage between the apartments. When music was played, on radio or cassette, it was loud, but people lived quietly. Perhaps, growing up in large families in few rooms, they expected to define their privacy by behaviour rather than by space. They rarely sat alone in a room, never slept alone, whether on the big bed or on a mat unrolled on the floor. So when they were together, restraint operated, between the generations of an extended family and between the partners of an arranged marriage. Talk overheard from verandas and windows kept to a constant, subdued level. Visitors slipped in and out, the Muslim women like white shadows.

The day began in the light before dawn with the rustle of a twig broom. A woman bent double, sweeping in the passage. The sound was rhythmic and light, the work an expenditure of time rather than physical effort, the levelling of dust that was never to be decisively swept away. The rustle came first from one direction and then another, as each household rose. It was followed by scraping and patting as uneven patches of path were tamped with a piece of wood; then the spatter of water thrown to dampen the dust; then silence, broken at intervals by the slap of feet in chappals passing the bedroom window as the compound prepared to bring in the day's water.

I got up around then. Though the sun had barely penetrated the passageway the view at its end was bright. Along Admiral Street, walls of turquoise and ochre had the morning clarity of colours in an Egyptian painting. Movement of people with pitchers on Admiral Street signified when our water was coming.

The temporary arrangements had been set up a good year before, when the damage first appeared in the water tank. They were expected to continue at least as long. Water was supplied from the big tank at Porayar, issuing from the pipes by the compound gate for a short period at some point between six and seven each morning. In other parts of the village it ran earlier; in some, later. I imagined a man at Porayar in mischievous control of the taps. The standpipes lay rather than stood, two or three feet below ground level. Outside our house, as along all the main streets of the village, trenches had been dug to just below the open mouth of the pipe. You put a basin beneath this, and, squatting in the hole, swiftly bailed the water into pitchers. A little technique had to be learned: because the earth was sandy the bottom of the trench was constantly filling and having to be scooped out; the sides crumbled further if you put a foot wrong, dirtying the basin; if you were too slow, the clean water overflowed from the basin and muddied; too late, and there was a puddle to be bailed out before you could begin. Then the pitchers were heavy, though old Indian women seemed to carry them with ease, and if you walked too fast holding one against your hip the water slopped out down your legs.

When there were heavy rains the supply was more perverse than usual. One morning late in December the water came for just a few minutes in the middle of a monsoon downpour, running directly into the puddles at the base of the trenches. That was all. Around lunchtime, after the storm had ceased, rainwater gushed suddenly from an overflow pipe on the roof and we raced out and caught a bucketful. Wilson had a man come round with a water tank on a bullock cart from which we filled up pitchers for washing, for a few rupees. A devilish water god grinned on the back of the tank; the man said that the water was good for drinking but I had seen him on other days drawing it from the well at the parade ground. Then at four in the afternoon Indra spotted water again trickling from the standpipe and everyone rushed out from their houses, gleeful as if manna were falling, to fill every available receptacle. Only then in the laughter did it become clear how they too, though apparently so patient, found the system irksome.

Three months later, just before I left Tranquebar, a man came one day and made connections to the pipes in our houses. He explained nothing. But the next morning, as if by a miracle, the sweet water from Porayar gushed directly into the troughs in our yards. Why had this not happened before? The rest of the village continued to bail its water out of holes.

Around seven in the morning the milkman came, riding a bicycle with a brass churn on the rack at the back, brass measures hanging from its side. He would sell an eighth, a quarter or half a litre, careful always to top up the measure with an extra drop, tipping the bicycle to one side to empty the churn by the tap at its base. From then until around nine, when the newspaper slapped on to the stone floor, the passageway echoed with the singsong English of the schoolboys who came to Wilson for tuition. They crowded his narrow veranda, three or four on chairs, others cross-legged on the ground, in blue shorts and pressed white shirts. Their textbooks were ancient beneath layers of annotation; the reading passages – Lesson Six, Toynbee on Nehru – history in themselves.

Through the rest of the day, hawkers passed, calling out at the gate. Salesmen came on bicycles loaded with bamboo mats, cottons and saris, tinkers with metal vessels mushrooming behind their backs, making an optical clatter in the sun. At weekends a sweetseller came from a village near Karikal carrying a huge pan of the melting glutinous sweets he had cooked that morning, which he sliced and weighed on the scales he carried and wrapped in leaves. He was some kind of protégé of Wilson's, possibly a former pupil, and had been doing the rounds of the villages with his sweets for twelve years though he still looked little more than a boy. Women came on foot carrying wide baskets of fish or vegetables on their heads. The deal was done on the doorstep, then the woman asked you to help her lift the basket back on to her head and you felt its weight. Once I said as much to Regina Mary, and how the crone who sold us onions must be at least sixty, but Regina Mary said no, she could be no more than forty-five.

Like all our neighbours, we had a servant. Shivaharmi was found for us by Sister Nirmala. She was old, thin, with wiry grey hair and a tight-pursed mouth that revealed a few betel-stained teeth if she smiled, but that did not happen often since she was sour as a pickle. Sister Nirmala said she brought her to us because she was a sincere person. Her husband was bedridden and they lived in the hut she had built for them in the waste ground between the remains of the Danish ramparts and the old port. Unfortunately we began by paying her at an exorbitant rate: Sister Nirmala seemed to consider it her duty to extract as much as she could from foreigners whom she knew were millionaires. As all our financial dealings were made public through the village this became a cause of some embarrassment.

'You are cooking yourself?' women asked in horror. I would explain that Tom needed Western-style food, but in their eyes I could see that it was a lame excuse. 'You do not understand these people. The more that you give your servant the less she will do.'

They seemed to be right. Shivaharmi came and went like a ghost. At first she brought in the water, which was what Sister Nirmala had arranged for her to do, but each day she came a little later and worked more slowly. Some days she came so late that we had brought it in ourselves before she arrived. She rubbed her back and said that she had stomach pains and that a day before the doctor in Porayar had given her injections in both arms (injections were her universal panacea). Then she said that it was heavy work and she was old, all of which was true, and she had first to bring in her own water, a longer walk since there was no outlet by the thorn gate of her mud hut.

Guilty at having demanded so much of her, I went to Sheikh Allaud-din, who lent one of his men. All that was left for Shivaharmi, for her monthly three hundred rupees, was to sweep and to wash the clothes and vessels. She scratched by our feet with her twig broom at break-fast. Once weekly she washed the floor by pouring buckets of water on to it and swilling it about, leaving puddles that Tom slipped in, and that had not evaporated even by evening. In the yard she covered the washing with a lather of Surf then slapped it against the concrete; she was reluctant to do much rinsing, presumably since rinsing used up water. The vessels she arranged about her, and the crows came and ate the scraps off them. She put them to soak then rubbed them vaguely with sandy grains of Indian washing powder. Tom watched her and she watched him as if he were a strange animal. When I asked if she had children, her hands made the Indian gesture for no, cupped palms rolled up and then down to signify emptiness.

I tried to reform her. Wilson, who had begun by acting as interpreter between us, finally threw up his hands and said he would speak to her no more. She made him too angry. She was haughty. But in the next breath he reminded me that good servants were hard to find nowadays: 'We must be patient with these people or they will vanish and we shall have to do the work ourselves.' ASR had employed Shivaharmi previously. The old pastor was philosophical. 'That is human nature. If we pay extra, treat a servant well, she will

101

become haughty. If you give them your shirt they will take your pants.'

So Shivaharmi was sacked. ASR provided a replacement, a woman called Rajeswari who had been helping in his house while his permanent servant made a visit to her village. I paid her only two hundred rupees, still way above the usual rate but then I was a foreigner and because of my strange diet I did not require her to cook nor provide meals as did other employers.

Rajeswari kept ostentatiously busy. She jumped for the cobwebs and when she washed the vessels she taught Tom to caw back at the crows. She was small, not five foot, and cattishly pretty. Her laugh tinkled and her smile was catching. But sometimes her animation grated. When her face fell still, its lines relaxed into hardness and I was reminded just how rich I was to her and how much she might hope for from me.

On one of her first days I had her clean and cut some fish. When she left she took with her an empty baby-milk tin I had given her – the tin sealed with a plastic lid and I knew how Shivaharmi had valued my supply of containers. As Rajeswari went by my chair she let me see that the lid was open and that she had the fish heads inside.

'What are you going to do with those?' As if it were not obvious.

'Cook them.' Her grin turned on as if fish heads were a treat.

I gave her one of my fish as well. And in future I always bought an extra fish for her. It was nothing to me yet I was uncomfortable at the way she had contrived the gift.

The relationship was strange to me. Perhaps inequality embarrasses the English, so we have contrived our complex of formal barriers to conceal it. The Indian pattern is different. Not only is the gulf between mistress and servant exposed, it seems to be played upon. I felt that some return performance was required of me, a performance whose condescension made me uneasy, yet which would perhaps, in Indian terms, give dignity to both sides. It was a while before I could do the same as Tom and take Rajeswari's smile at face value.

At first, Regina Mary did not trust her either. She came to me discreetly and told me that her father advised against employing

Rajeswari. It was said in the village that she was not a good woman. I must watch carefully over my things.

Rajeswari had never been formally married but had a ten-year-old son. His father had not been seen for years. She had no house but camped behind a thorn fence by the path that ran up to the gate of the old temple at the heart of the village. She showed me her home one day – again with a self-consciousness that seemed to require something of me but which I felt I must ignore at least until the moment I left Tranquebar.

For most of its length the road, which turned off by ASR's house, was unpopulated, bounded only by high garden walls. It was against one of these that she had set her thorn fence. The gate, which was also woven from thorn branches, was fastened with a cheap padlock; some months before someone had broken in and stolen all her saris. To one end of her strip of territory was a screen of thorn and palm leaf; behind this was her washing place, the water draining on to a couple of seedling banana trees. Over most of the remaining area a roof of palmleaf matting was raised on poles to give shade and at the end she had built a mud lean-to, again flimsily locked, where she kept her bed-roll and remaining clothes – stifling to sleep in normally but relatively dry in the rains, if she made a bed of planks raised above the wet earth.

Regina Mary was a good Catholic girl. She might not have mentioned if Rajeswari's reputation had some cause other than stealing. There were not many options for a single mother without family, squatting in a backstreet in a place like Tranquebar. Prostitution was the first which sprang to mind.

ASR was almost her closest neighbour. Recently he had begun to take an interest in her and give her Bible instruction. Her son had gone as a boarder to a TELC children's home and she had joined a women's group run by the Mission. I heard that in the course of a meeting there she bit another woman's ear but I never found out why. A few months after returning to England I received a letter she had dictated to ASR to tell me that she had been baptised.

15

Light on bare feet, the girls sped from hall into bedroom, out through the second door that led to the corridor by the yard, and round again, then doubled back as Tom gave chase. Regina Mary hid behind one of the doors. A dark eye and a plait peeked out. She ran, giggling behind long fingers. When he caught her, the giggles turned to sobs. Puzzled, he tried to take her hands from her face, but fast as he grabbed one, the other replaced it over her closed eyelids, again and again, until all of a sudden both hands flew apart and brown eyes laughed at him. Another moment and behind him Indra too was crying, hiding her face in her hands. Or was that the edge of a smile in the gap between her fingers?

The games were repeated endlessly. He sat on the veranda between the little Muslim girls from next door. It was Marhin now who cried, shoulders shaking piteously. Her older sister Jebin started up beside her, and just as Tom's own face began to fold they dropped their hands in unison and the joke was revealed.

Other children played in the garden. There were the children of the other Muslim family: a sharp-faced girl and her brother Azaruddin, and their family servant, a Hindu girl of ten or twelve who swept and washed and prepared the food each day, and accompanied the daughter to the bus stand to see her off to her English-medium school on the edge of Karikal. Wilson's oldest son came with his family for Christmas, with a daughter the same age as Tom. And there was the baby Sherbin. Indian babies seemed quieter than English ones, carried about all day long, fed mouthfuls of rice and curd pressed between the fingers. An English missionary I met had a theory that it was this quietist diet that made them so undemanding.

Their existence was cocooned within the compound walls. It seemed a long way from the hard India of the streets. In Regina

Mary's care, Tom rarely went out even into the full sun. He played in the gloom of fanned rooms, the shade of the veranda and of the trees that overhung most of the garden.

Jebin and Marhin came and went through our open door. They slipped in silently, then took off again like butterflies. They were two years apart in age, eight and six. They had pageboy haircuts and wore silver anklets whose little bells tinkled as they ran. Sometimes a line of kohl elongated their eyes or a painted beauty spot empha-sised a high cheekbone, and they flounced in wearing red lipstick and flourished their hands to show the hennaed patterns on the palms. Often they changed their clothes twice in a day. They had 'ready-mades' their father had brought from Singapore: lacy tights and high-collared Chinese blouses, and chiffon dresses of blue and yellow with pink silk roses sewn in at the waist. Other clothes were made by their mother and their aunts, who also painted their faces and pinned flowers in their hair. At seven in the morning they rushed off to mosque school, shawls over their heads and wooden bookrests folded under their arms. Around half past eight they came home for break-fast and at nine they picked up their slates and went to the Muslim primary school with a lesser sense of urgency.

Regina Mary teased them when they dawdled. 'To school,' she said, schoolmarmish herself. 'To school to school,' they sang back at her, and the English phrase became the cry of an owl. Regina Mary disapproved of the frivolity of Muslim girls. At the convent she had learnt to take education seriously: she intended to be able to support herself and to save towards her own dowry, for she did not expect to marry until late in her twenties.

'*Parangi kayai parithu*', the girls chanted Tamil rhymes in mechan-ical voices:

> Take a pumpkin from the plant
> Skin it all over and cut out the pith
> Chop it into little pieces
> Mix in a little salt
> And mix in chillies too
> Fry it in oil
> And eat it hot

Then ask for some more
If we get some we shall laugh
If we don't we shall cry,

Then there was a clapping song about rice and curd that repeated and repeated and accelerated into dervishry. They tried to teach it to Tom one afternoon up on the roof where they went to spy on the street and on the adjoining back yards.

They had few toys. They had their rhymes and finger games, they dressed up and threaded garlands, sitting crosslegged on the floor before a heap of flowers brought from someone's garden. When toys were needed they took what came to hand. All of one sultry morning in the late rains they played jacks with black pebbles picked from the rubble outside the house. They sat on the floor of the veranda in grey light; there was a power cut and a building storm showed in the gap between the roofs. In England we used to play the game with a rubber ball and metal jacks. It is harder with stones: there is no chance of a bounce when you throw one into the air, and stones do not lock so neatly when gathered in the palm of the hand.

One day the sun was strong when I came back to the house at noon. Jebin skipped up to meet me, her hair oiled and tied with December flowers that matched the mauve swirls in her frock. Tom was standing rapt at our gate as her older sister Shirin turned a mirror in the ray of sun that fell into the passage, glancing quicksilver pools of light along the shaded walls.

Shirin did not share in her sisters' coquetry. She was a quiet girl of seventeen, with a solemn oval face. At prayertimes she would unroll her mat in a corner of the living room, tie a shawl over her hair and go through her devotions, kneel and touch her head to the floor, while Jebin and Marhin chattered and their mother Yasmin sewed, and their grandmother observed it all through magnified eyes, seated on the floor with her back to the doorframe.

Often Yasmin would put on her fardtha, the voluminous white outer robe of the Muslim women, and take all the girls out on visits to cousins, leaving only her old mother curled on a mat with an arm across her face. Or cousins would come to them. Usually they paused

106

at our gate to get a glimpse of the English boy. Once I was cooking and Tom ran in and caught my hand.

'What is it, Tom? What do you want to show me?'

He pulled me through to the bedroom, and there were five faces pressed to the window grille, dark smiles framed in white veils.

The looks of the Muslim women could be very different from those of the Hindu Tamils. Some, like Jebin, had paler skin and longer features, more Aryan or more Arabic. Others looked Malay, and a few had oriental faces that surprised me until I learnt that they came from Vietnam, where Tranquebar Muslims used to trade. They and many of the older women wore instead of a sari a kind of sarong of batique cloth.

A daily visitor was the oldest of the four sisters, Bhanu, who had left school and gone to run her grandfather's household in Mosque Street. Often she came in to me. Sometimes I joined her at her mother's. There was calm there in the circle of women, through the piecemeal work of the afternoons, as hands folded thin pastry for parathas or rolled chappatis on a round wooden board. Bhanu was twenty, light skinned, tall and languorous. She often ran painted fingernails through her thick black hair. Touches of sophistication in her dress set her apart from Tranquebar and had been gleaned from foreign magazines. She spoke English well, in a throaty, measured voice.

My foreignness endowed me with unnatural glamour in her eyes. 'You know the world,' she would say. 'I like to talk with you. No one like you has come here before. You have done many things. And you only now have a baby although you are thirty-five.'

Most of the Muslim women she knew had married at eighteen, and those marriages had often been arranged a couple of years before. By the time they reached their thirties she thought them old, matrons with many children.

A visiting aunt looked on without comprehension, chin resting on her hands. She was little older than Bhanu, come from Chidambaram to show off her first child to her husband's relatives. The heavy gold jewellery she wore was part of her dowry, also on display – the jewellery that represented a married couple's wealth, that women

107

took to be weighed on the scales at the bank's loans counter when they got into debt.

Bhanu was not ready for all that. 'I say, I will have one child. Two at most. I am a modern girl.'

But she said that only to me. Within a year, she too was to have a marriage arranged. Her grandfather would contribute to the dowry in return for the work she had done at his house. Her father and her mother's brothers would choose her husband. Her father sent postcards from Singapore which were pinned to a door: glassy buildings against barren blue skies. She looked to them and lowered her voice.

'Now, in this day and age, I want to have some part in it. I want to meet my husband and talk with him before we are married, like Christian and Hindu girls. But I tell you truly, I want to marry from the heart. Better that you find a husband for me, an Englishman.'

Marriage would be a continuation of the life she led at her grandfather's, only more restricted. She would have to live with her mother-in-law and she would have less time to herself. At her grandfather's she liked to watch television and to listen to the cassettes that cousins sent from Paris. When she said Paris it sounded like chocolate.

I asked if she had friends at Tranquebar.

'A few,' she said, shaking her head ambiguously. 'Four. But not good friends, not like you. You talk frankly.'

'Then how do they talk? What do they talk about?'

'What they make for lunch, what they wear. Yesterday one came. She told me that a good Muslim girl should not wear a T-shirt like the one I have from France, not even inside the house. It shows the body. But I like it, black with just a little pattern, Parisian.'

'And what else do they say?'

'Oh, nothing. They play. They do not live from the heart.'

Yasmin once showed me the family photographs – few, but prized, and kept on a high shelf in the wardrobe in the bedroom. Half a dozen took each girl through her childhood: from fat baby with big eyes ringed in kohl and beauty spots on her cheeks, to pretty toddler and dark Lolita. Bhanu was the most beautiful all the way through. In one photograph, aged perhaps twelve, she posed coolly with her back to a gilt-edged mirror. Her dress was of some satiny fabric, primrose yellow, with a tight bodice and a tiered skirt like a Spanish dancer's; her eyes were made up, her forehead decorated with a diamanté star, her wide lips painted scarlet and her hair drawn back, the mirrored reflection showing how it was threaded behind with jasmine flowers.

Her growing up seemed a progress towards inevitable disappointment. The days were charmed for little Muslim girls. They need only dress, play, laugh beautifully. Even school required little discipline since little was expected of them there. But from puberty onwards their world narrowed, from the moment they began to menstruate and first had to cover themselves in public. The fardtha was prettier than the black robe of Arab women – usually of light white cotton, scalloped and embroidered at the edges – but enveloping none the less.

'Pah!' said Bhanu. 'I do not like to wear the fardtha. It gets in the way and it is hot: yards and yards of it.'

16

A walk on up Queen Street from the colony passed between old houses with wooden pillars and verandas on platforms raised a few steps above the dust. A few doors along, a baby often slept in a hammock of rose-coloured cotton strung from a beam by the door. There was little traffic: a couple of bullock carts, as many bicycles, a rare car causing a boy to stare, halting with his stick the old bicycle tyre he used as a hoop. People walked down the centre of the street even when the sun was hottest, as the north–south axis allowed no shade.

At the junction with Mosque and Goldsmith Streets, one or two men stood at a tea stand. From there came the dungy odour of the bidis they smoked. Opposite were shops: a couple of skullcapped grocers hunched on their platforms before blackened scales, and a tailor at his treadle machine beneath a picture of Mecca. Mosque Street was exclusively Muslim, running up to the mosque which lay at the edge of a field containing a large tank, close to the old ramparts and the moat; old maps of Tranquebar show a mosque on this site though they mark the garden separately and describe it as the Admiral's Garden. A new mosque was in course of construction, modernistically white amongst the sun-worn dilapidation. It was to be a tight-run thing whether the mosque or the Zion Church restoration, both scheduled for completion in March, would be inaugurated first.

The house where Bhanu lived was built to the traditional plan despite the art deco 1954 on the concrete façade. The central courtyard was cool beneath a tiled roof supported on painted wooden columns, light falling only through the small open square at the centre. Various rooms rambled off at the sides but it was there in the courtyard that the occupants of the house met, before the unclosing eye of the television.

When I took coffee there with her grandfather this was tuned to

some educational programme on engineering; a commentary smat-
tered with English technical terms irrelevantly filled the pauses in
conversation. The old man lay with his feet up on a planter's chair.
Since all the other chairs were upright this gave him subliminal domi-
nance. He was unshaven, a thin white stubble on his chin. He had
fine features and light skin like the girls, nothing Tamil in his looks.
He said the family had been in Tranquebar four hundred years, and
waved his hand at the darkness behind his shoulder where the
refrigerator buzzed, so vague that the four hundred seemed a figure
pulled from air.

'We belong at Tranquebar. We all return here. I spent many years
in Vietnam, trading.' He spoke in slurred French. 'My business was
textiles, cottons and silks, local, French and Indian. It was good. But
even if there had been no war I would have returned.'

His age made me wonder for a moment whether he meant the war
with the French or that with the Americans. But then he introduced
his youngest son, who was no more than twenty – little older than
Bhanu his granddaughter – and had a smooth oriental face that
showed Vietnamese blood. The old man had taken a second wife and
had a second family at Saigon while the first remained at Tranquebar.
The boy was shortly to leave for Paris, where his three half-brothers
were already working, two in trade and one a doctor. The pattern of
overseas work continued, though that of return to Tranquebar must
be becoming less and less assured.

Past the Muslim section the streets began to peter out, up to the
line of the north wall of which not a stone remained in place. Queen
Street ended in an open square before the fisherpeople's temple, a
modern temple, coarsely made and painted, that served also as a
meeting house and court where disputes could be settled without
reference to the law outside. After the square, dirt road narrowed
and curled into path, winding between fences of woven thorn that
had dried to the same dust colour as the beaten earth. Thorn gates
opened into dirt compounds, the monotony of colour broken by the
reddish terracotta of storage jars, by the occasional turquoise wash
on a low mud wall beneath a pitched roof of palm thatch, or by the
feathers of a scratching cockerel.

111

This was the fishermen's quarter, crowded and poor. I rarely went there since it was impossible to walk alone. Even when I was familiar through the rest of Tranquebar, I had only to step among the fishermen's houses to draw a band of children, chased by first one voice, and then another, and then a raucous chorus, 'What is your name?' and 'Paise, Paise!' – the latter cry become a senseless chant, unaccompanied by outstretched hand or expectation of money. So I would turn away through increasingly shambolic paths towards the breath of the sea, breaking at last into its dazzle, rid of my retinue as I scrambled down a bank of sand.

The northern beach stretched half a mile or more, from the shore temple to a rivermouth before which stood a plain shrine and a terracotta horse. It was broad and dull, pale sand streaked with black. In the mornings especially it was sordid, when a chain of figures squatted before the incoming waves and left piles of excrement lined up every yard along the strand. Along the first section, where the village was closest, scores of catamarans were pulled up and the day's catch was brought in. Up on the dry sand the nets were disentangled and spread, and the women gathered to sort and trade the shivering fish, packing them into wide baskets, sprinkling each layer with sand and covering them with a folded cloth. Their flapping saris were always shadowed by the dark wings of crows and kites, which swooped within arm's length for whatever was discarded.

The fisherpeople often had as many as nine children. At Porayar Dr Chandrasekaran and his wife Dr Parvati offered contraception. But the moment they pushed it or began to lecture, their patients left them. They witnessed birth after birth, saw the child healthy for the first year or two as long as it was breastfed, then fall prey to skin diseases and diarrhoea – the results of ignorance and bad sanitation. The Chandrasekarans said that the diseases were accepted as heaven sent and left to take their course. It was the Hindu way. Educated brahmins, they despaired.

And the Muslim way, they said, was 'What God wills'. The Muslims left it to God to give them children or not. So many of their families were as large as the fisherpeople's and most of the Muslims of Tranquebar were poor. It was not possible to teach a mother the care of her child since this was dictated by the older women. Parvati had attended births where forty women relatives had crowded into a single small room, terrifying the woman in labour with their shrieked advice. 'What can a simple doctor do before such power? At first I yelled back at them: shut up, go away! But now I'm used to it. I don't expect to change things now.'

In the little maternity hospital behind St Theresa's convent, the number of beds was to be doubled. Sister Cicely who ran the hospital spoke in a rapid burble that echoed her mother tongue, Malayalam. 'We now have fourteen births a month. This year more than last year, last year more than the year before, and I know already that next year will be more than this year. A single ward is no longer enough.'

The facilities she had were clean but basic. The green metal beds were ranged barely two foot apart beneath a row of fans in the narrow ward. A bare cubicle at the end was reserved for labour, with next to it a latrine and washroom. The arrangement was to be repeated for the extension.

No one in the village could have been more aware of the need for family planning. As Roman Catholics the nuns could not support the use of contraceptives and instead they energetically promoted natural birth control, going out to teach the women of the various communities. Sister Cicely admitted it seemed a little quixotic. 'Even for educated people the success rate is not good. And the fisherfolk . . . The fishermen work hard, they go out in their boats, they mend their nets, their lives are short and they see their wives for just a moment in the night. What do you think happens? They are men and they forget.

'Our task is really to teach responsibility. What is the size of the English family?'

I said I thought the average was around two children.

'So people are more responsible there?'

The hospital also contained a dispensary, an examination room and a waiting room where there were always fresh flowers in the vase at the feet of a plaster Virgin. A new mother came in shyly; eighteen was the legal minimum age for marriage but she looked younger.

113

Her baby was six weeks old and his feet were deformed, twisted inwards at the ankle. Sister Cicely manipulated them regularly. She said that this was not an uncommon deformity but that his was a particularly bad case. She rubbed oil into the skin.

'The ankles feel more flexible already. See, I can bend them a little way; that was not possible before. When the boy is three months they will be put in a plaster cast.'

The feet were still nowhere near straight. I asked if it would work and he would learn to walk.

'I will make it work. If the plaster cast is not successful there is a surgeon we can see.' She handed the baby back to his mother. 'He is very important to her. He is a son and he is her firstborn.'

Around his wrists he wore bracelets of dry pieces of garlic threaded on a string. Sister Cicely said this was to ward off disease.

'Perhaps it helps. More likely, it keeps insects away. The people here are very superstitious. A mother will stay in the post-natal ward for five, seven, nine, eleven or so days. Even if she and the baby are thriving she will leave only on days with odd numbers.'

Born a Catholic into the large Christian community of the state of Kerala, with a sister at a convent in Rome, brisk and rational, she was as bemused by Hindu superstition as she was by the complex caste relationships of Tamil Nadu.

17

The village made me frugal. It came to seem conspicuous consumption to leave a light on or let the fan continue to run when I left a room. Others sat in semi-darkness in their homes, turning on the light and the fan in the same way they brought out the obligatory metal chair, as a courtesy when I came to visit.

Though I went by bus to the market in Karikal I sometimes took an autorickshaw back: hard enough to squeeze on to an Indian bus with bags of shopping on one arm and a child on the other, let alone burst out in one piece at the other end. But we were seen, even if I told the auto to stop before the bus stand instead of taking it to the door; and the Pondicherry Territory licence made it clear where we had come from. 'Three times you have come from Karikal by autorickshaw,' someone would say. 'Why do you do this? You know that the bus costs only one rupee forty?'

The journey by auto squandered the best part of forty rupees, just over a pound, more than two days' wages for many Indians. The local rate for agricultural labourers at harvest time was about sixteen rupees a day for men, twelve for women. Knowing that, you could make sense of a newspaper item about a dacoity on the Bombay–Bhagalpur Express, when dacoits threatened passengers but required each one to produce no more than twenty rupees. For travellers in the unreserved second-class carriages where the dacoits struck, this was a meaningful sum. Cash was even scarcer in a southern, rural community like Tranquebar, where cardamom pods were so costly that the grocer priced them individually, and people shredded the sides of the leaves on their banana trees because perfect leaves got stolen, for sale to restaurants as plates – and every leaf counted since it was reckoned that the number of bunches a banana tree produced was in direct relation to the number of leaves.

I found it more discreet to walk or cycle the mile to the shops at

Porayar. I went either along the road or through the fields, along the rutted track that ran past the abandoned station and the row of empty one-room railway houses by the line.

Porayar was much larger than Tranquebar, with state-run hospital and schools, a bus terminus and a small market. It was a rambling place without Tranquebar's colonial form, just a 'native village' or 'suburb' in the *British Imperial Gazetteers*. But the Danes had given it one of their fine archways, which stood now in the press of the market street, a dark gate leading into a garden which was called the Nadar Garden or the Company's Garden. This covered a couple of acres in the heart of the village, a walled rectangle quartered by paths, at its centre a colonial house and a great tank.

The garden had been let go, the palms springing clear from a thorny tangle. The house was white and classical with columns and urn-topped balustrades. A veranda ran the breadth of the front. Originally there would have been cane jalousies hung between the columns but now a pitched awning of palm thatch kept the sun out. The flat roof above made a generous balcony for the first floor, where full-length windows were closed by flaking brown shutters.

There was always someone lurking in the veranda twilight. On my first visit I met three men and from a jumble of English began to collect fragments of the story of the house. One said that twenty-five people currently lived there, six family groups in six rooms on the ground floor, all of them Nadars. Another, that in the old days they had owned a British car, a Standard convertible. He showed the photograph to prove it, framed on the veranda wall. The third told how when Nadar reunions were held three hundred members of the clan gathered there, from the surrounding district, from Tirunelveli in the south of Tamil Nadu, and from Madras.

The men were brothers or cousins. Between them, they ran a shop, collected the rents of a village, and managed a small farm with six labourers; yet none of these occupations was so demanding that they need leave the shade on a bright morning. Their grandfather – no, perhaps they meant their great-grandfather – had been an arrack king, a great landowner whose estates had ranged from Kerala to Jaipur. It was he who had bought the garden from the British and built the house, in the 1850s. The King of Tanjore had once been his guest.

They took me down a corridor hung with hunting trophies into a high durbar hall. It was airless though it rose a clear storey above the rest of the house. Wires that once held punkahs dangled uselessly from the distant ceiling. The first row of windows, that might have let a draught through from the upper floor, were shuttered. The second row above them, of coloured glass, showed the sky only through broken panes and threw drops of topaz and burgundy light into the well below. The Nadar ancestors stared overhead. There was the old man they called the founder, Velliya Nadar, with a Mexican bandit's moustache, in prime position opposite the main entrance. Above the door to his left a stern face was all but obscured by varnish and gloom; this they said was Thavasumuthu Nadar, but an elision of syllables made it sound like 'the thousandth Nadar' which would have been suitably dynastic. Oil paintings gave way to monochrome studio photographs and these were replaced by informal twentieth-century shots. The man who drove the Leyland in the picture on the veranda reappeared in group photographs in other rooms: square jaw, bags under his eyes, double-breasted suit, he posed with his British friends the Carltons in Madras.

The floors were gritty though the walls had recently been white-washed. Only the six inhabited rooms were swept and only one of these escaped the touch of neglect, a woman's room with pink walls and dark carved furniture. The room next to it held evidence of fashionable refurbishment in the 1930s: a cupboard with mirrored panels and a large pre-war wireless inserted in the wall. Had the '30s been the family's heyday, the period of the motor car? Upstairs, the shutters were veiled with cobwebs and the floors were littered with cigarette ends. Odd pieces of furniture had been pushed to the side to make room for heaps of grain. One landing was carpeted with earth, home to four white rabbits, and on the balcony flat cakes of cow dung were laid out in the sun as in a peasant's yard.

I drank tea with one of the men as his wife fed Tom Britannia brand Bourbon biscuits. He spoke of times before Independence. The hunting trophies in the corridor were from before. 'Before, people from London went hunting with my father, and my grandfather, at

Tirunelveli.' The British had also come to Porayar, and to his cousin's house on the beach at Tranquebar. 'Before, London people came, drinking and eating. In the bungalow by the seashore, in one room there was a special wooden floor for dancing. London people liked to dance.'

The seashore bungalow had intrigued me from my first sight of it, ten years previously. At last I met someone who arranged to take me there. Maya Sekar was a cousin of the men at the Company's Garden and of those who lived at the bungalow. She herself had been born at Tranquebar, in a colonial house that had lost almost every vestige of Danishness, remodelled a little each time it was damaged in the rains.

The house on the shore had also been remodelled. I remembered how it was before: how the nineteenth-century villa had been encircled by tiered arcades of veranda and balcony; how the broken lattice that yawned from the upper arches and the fallen sections of parapet reflected the desertion of the colonial village on that leaden June day; how the waves spilled towards the little cliff where the garden crumbled suddenly into beach. Both balcony and parapet were now gone. Even the long shutters had been taken from the windows, which were filled instead with concrete fretwork. The walls of the first floor stood exposed beneath the flat roof, looking blankly out to the beach and the parade ground.

Maya said that an additional wing running out into the garden had also been demolished. I did not remember this but a double line of truncated columns showed where it had run through the coconuts towards the beach. The resale of bricks and wood had brought in three lakhs of rupees.

The house had been built some time before the Danes left Tranquebar. The *Imperial Gazetteers* list it as the former Collector's bungalow and the residence of the judge during court sessions, and as the finest house in the district, adding helpfully that it belonged to a native gentleman who might make it available for the use of European officers and travellers. The widow who now owned the house said that the Madras governor had stayed there in 1921. Her father-in-law had presented him with an ivory-handled walking stick which she believed to be now in a London museum.

In a bedroom on the ground floor stood a huge tarnished looking-glass in a mahogany frame. An old electric fan rested on a table whose legs ran down from carved elephant heads. Heavy furniture filled corners and jammed passageways, coated like the red floors with sand. The main rooms led off each side of a long central hall, and a passage ran through to the kitchen, past a puja room like a closet hung with a fine old painting of Krishna riding a white bull. The original kitchen had been evacuated when its roof began to fall in. They cooked instead in a storeroom, the walls of which were already black with smoke. They had moved a heavy wooden dresser in there but did not use it. The cooking vessels were piled on the floor.

Peasant house was reclaiming colonial mansion, the function of rooms and furniture apparently forgotten. From doors to the left of the hall a shallow staircase wound up to what had been the ballroom. The last great parties had been held forty years before, when three sons were married at once; the celebrations went on for three days. There was indeed a fine wooden floor, and the ceiling rose to double height. Ceiling and walls kept remnants of plaster mouldings and panels, though bats hung between the beams. Louvred doors gave on to side rooms that would once have opened to the balcony and the sea breeze. These rooms were empty, save one where a line was stretched for drying clothes. On the floor lay an open suitcase with papers scattered around it as if someone had just fled: another token of the family's amnesia, for I saw that the strewn envelopes bore postmarks from the 1950s.

At the end of the ballroom we looked down the passage which led to the original sleeping apartments, currently occupied by another section of the family. Straw was spread across the floor there between the columns, for cattle which had been brought in during the rains.

Maya translated what the widow told me. 'She says that forty years back the state government wanted to buy the house for tourism. Officials came to look around and said that they could make a fine hotel. But her father-in-law did not sell. The Nadars had owned the house for generations. Others would not care for it.'

Sheikh Allauddin however had whispered that they would now be prepared to sell, to the right offer, and the structure of the building since the alterations was generally thought to be sound.

The widow, whose name was Rajeswari Thavasumuthu Nadar, shared the house with her two sons and their families. I had seen her often at the gate when I passed on the way to the beach, a strong-looking woman with thick grey hair, herding passive grand-children and hostile dogs. We drank coffee at the table in the hall downstairs. A couple of sparrows had been caught in the room and they flitted beneath the ceiling. The pictures on the stained blue walls included the usual ancestral photographs and a couple of framed goddesses, Sarasvati with peacock and vina, Lakshmi on a lotus, paper prints densely appliquéd with fragments of silk, gold thread and sequins. They had been made by her mother-in-law, a relic of the days when the Nadar ladies spent their time at handicrafts.

Her father-in-law had been an eminent man. She brought from a cupboard under Sarasvati his British India passport, issued in 1924: V. Balagurusamy Nadar. And she produced a wilted Danish magazine in which he was interviewed. She said that it was he who had insti-gated the visit of the Danish Prime Minister. But he had presided over decline. The only business remaining to the house was the sale of seashells. Rajeswari Thavasumuthu had inherited the sole licence for the village, which the family had held for the past sixty years. The monopoly covered all the shells gathered on the Tranquebar beaches, which were purchased from the fishing women and resold in bulk to be powdered for whitewash. 'It is a good business,' she told Maya. 'We buy the shells from very poor people.' But the profits were no longer good enough to cover the cost when the licence had come up for renewal three years before, and the Nadars on the seashore now held only a third share.

The sea itself had added to their losses. We walked in the garden towards the beach. When she left school fifteen years earlier, Maya could remember a hundred and twenty coconuts between the bunga-low and the shore. Only twenty-one palms remained. Maya pointed down the drop where the land ended, to the bricks and tumbled columns littering the strand, and the encircling parapet from the well that had stood at the centre of the plantation. Thirty yards to the left, the stone foundations of the temple had held out against the waves better than the soft soil of the garden. She said she could remember when the temple was intact, as she could also remember the Company's Garden trimmed and weeded when she went as a child to swim in the tank. Her father had told her that when he was a boy, forty or fifty years before, the sea was so far off that the family used to take their tiffin out by bullock cart when they went to the beach.

Ruin was a condition of Tranquebar's existence. The Coromandel coast was eroded with every monsoon, beaten by the storms and by the strong currents that raced down at that season from the north-east, and it was eroded most markedly along the Cauvery delta where the soft alluvium was washed away faster than it could now accumulate. The Danish fort was originally built two hundred metres from the water's edge. That distance had slimmed to less than fifty. As long ago as 1681, a typhoon caused the sea to flood the fort and half of the bulwarks fell. By 1775, such a large portion of the Danes' original territory had been lost that they attempted, unsuccessfully, to secure a further grant of land, first by request to the King of Tanjore and later by military force. In the nineteenth century, great typhoons were recorded in 1849 and 1871, and the British adminis-tration constructed extensive breakwaters to protect the town, the remains of which now jutted vainly from the waves. In recent memory, a damaging typhoon had occurred in every decade: 1952, 1961, 1977, 1985.

18

Wilson worked in his patch of garden, tying up the frame for a rose arbour. It looked a struggle. A jungle had grown in the few months of the rains.

'We have to be very dedicated now to our gardening. We shall have to bring all the water to our plants. We must carry it to the plants each morning. You will see, two weeks of January have passed now and no more rain will come.'

'But Wilson, you said before that it never rained after the end of December.' Not a drop, he had said, the climate kept a very strict timetable. He had repeated the prediction after the heavy rainfall of the first week of January.

'Ah, this is irregular.' He winced. 'And here I am being scratched by thorns and stung by ants. These little ants are stinging me as I work!'

That morning his forecast was believable. The sunlight struck white against the sheets that dried on the line.

On the roof of the neighbouring house, the bare figures of two labourers stood against the sky. Demolition work had started again. For days on end all was quiet at the house, and then the hammering would set up once more and a loaded cart would be seen turning from the gate, or a man carrying a beam on his shoulder, in slow motion under its weight. They had just begun on the roof. The two men worked sporadically, pounding at the concrete with iron poles, then scraping at the loosened rubble with rough tools, putting up puffs of dust like smoke signals.

The Chandrasekarans introduced me to another Nadar who was a neighbour of theirs, a tall woman, rather fine and severe in a plain cotton sari of faded crimson. Doctor Chandrasekaran interpreted since she spoke scarcely a word of English – only the epithet 'the founder' which was attached to her distant ancestor Velliya Nadar. According to her, Velliya's son was Thavasumuthu, and Thavasumuthu himself had three sons: one was still living, the head of the family and occupant of the Company Garden house; the two others had owned the seashore bungalow and the house on King Street. I tried to dovetail this with what Maya had told me about the family and decided that there must have been a fourth brother, perhaps a half-brother, who was her father; later I realised that a generation had been skipped as well. The Nadar family tree, like the rest of local history, was loosely kept.

The woman said that it was Velliya Nadar who had made the family rich. Before that, the Nadars had been simple coolies, toddy tappers whose job it was to collect from the palm trees the sap from which toddy was made.

Dr Chandrasekaran went on. 'So, this woman says that early one morning, Velliya Nadar went out as usual to the trees and by chance discovered buried treasure, not a kilometre's distance from Porayar. He found a hoard of gold coins, which he took directly to the Europeans. As his reward the Europeans gave him the three finest houses in the district. And from being a toddy tapper he became a great arrack maker.'

'Did it really happen like that?'

Dr Chandrasekaran shook his head noncommittally. 'They are country people here, they have many stories. And we have lived here so long that we also begin to believe them.

'I can tell you that when we first came to Porayar fifteen years ago, the Company's Garden house seemed a palace. But already one section has fallen down. The family is losing its fortune. The sons do no work. They do not even make investments. They know only how to draw money from the bank. They may be rich but they are ignorant.'

He gave his version of the story of the thirty-five-year-old man who had died at the Nadar house on King Street following an attack of chickenpox. It turned out that the family had eventually swallowed their fear of the goddess Mariamman and called a doctor, but only in the final stage of the illness. Chandrasekaran had visited immediately and diagnosed what he called chickenpox encephalitis. He recognised how close the man was to inevitable death and rushed him to hospital, but his aim by then was no more than to get the patient off his hands before he expired and thus to protect his practice in the village.

The Nadar woman took me to meet the head of the family. On the way we paused before her own house, where she put on her chappals: though she might cross the road in bare feet, she would not go like that to the Company's Garden. At the door of the uninhabited hall she left off her chappals and I did likewise, then a servant ushered us through the dust to the rooms in the east wing where T. G. Ratnasamy Nadar lived. There was time for no more than an introduction, for he had an appointment in Mayuram; a driver waited outside in a cream Ambassador.

T. G. Ratnasamy must have been around seventy, a biggish man even so, with thick grey hair and somewhat heavy features resembling those of the young motorist in the photographs. His apparent forcefulness was curbed by punctilious courtesy, and a quiet manner that owed something to British expression and gesture and must have been acquired alongside his knowledge of the English language. He was one of the few people I met locally who carried the imprint of the British era and thus made me conscious of my own Britishness, as happened often in the cities and among more educated communities in India.

He invited me to tea at four o'clock the following Thursday. We walked together through the hall and I stopped at the threshold to put on my shoes. He corrected me. 'But there was no need to remove your shoes here. Please, I am aware how things are done in England.'

When I went to tea I came in on a business meeting. Perhaps I was early, more likely he was running late. He lay with his feet up on the bed in his room, checking a sheaf of broad white papers that looked like legal documents. He seemed far more Indian than at the first meeting. He took his time to fold the papers and return them to a steel deed box which lay on the window sill. His associate, whom I took to be his lawyer, scanned a piece in the newspaper before taking desultory leave.

The room was the one where I had noticed the old wireless. Its walls were powdery green and the lower half of the window was of frosted blue glass, turning the colour to turquoise. The upper casement was open, giving a view of palms across which a stray thread of bougainvillea wavered. The few furnishings were of dark wood, the cover on the bed densely patterned. A couple of shirts and dhotis hung from a wooden rack on one wall; a blue fibreglass suitcase containing papers and a closed steel trunk lay on the floor. Behind the door, in the corner between the wall and the bed, was a low table for puja. Propped up on it were framed images in fairground colours: Shiva and Shakti, androgynous as babies, and Ganesh. A lush heap of jasmine and scarlet hibiscus flowers lay before the oil lamp.

T. G. Ratnasamy opened one of the mirrored doors set in the wall behind the bed, took out a crisp banknote and sent a servant to buy coffee and cakes. One of his sons came in to join us, a man with a thin moustache and a neat red pinpoint painted on his forehead. He took up a cup to rinse it and opened one of the glass-panelled doors; I had a glimpse of the adjoining bathroom installed in the thirties, with fittings that were still rarities in Porayar.

My host had prepared for our meeting as for an interview. He picked up from the bed a page of scribbled notes on the family history. It was a page of headed paper in the colonial style, with headings for date and camp in the top right-hand corner. As we talked he referred to these frequently. He read a snatch, then branched off, going back when he found that he had rambled from his place in the narrative. Sometimes he looked to them for a word that he wanted, catching up a phrase, repeating it for effect or when he liked the English. His son listened, corrected occasionally and prompted, stretched across the foot of the wooden bed.

'Our history begins with one Perumalsamy Nadar who was a native of S—, a village in Thirunelveli district. He and his brothers were the petty chiefs of some villages around there. As a result of a quarrel between the brothers, Perumalsamy Nadar left the place with his family and settled down at Porto Novo which is in South Arcot district. As he found no bright future for him there, he left that place also and finally settled down at Porayar which is in Tanjore district.

125

At that time Porayar, Tranquebar and some other villages are under the rule of Dutch people.' A wave of the hand covered that colonial period. 'A son was born to Perumalsamy Nadar when he was at Porto Novo, by the name of Velliya Nadar, who was the founder of the Nadar estate.

'Velliya Nadar became a contractor for toddy and arrack shops. There is a difference between these two liquors, you know: toddy comes directly from the palm while arrack is made up with jaggery and other ingredients. Velliya Nadar was a clever man and good with his hands. It is said – but I tell you this off the record, you know, because it is not verified – it is said that once the Dutch governor had a very painful boil on his neck, and that Velliya Nadar came and lanced it for him. It was thus that he gained the governor's friendship . . . Well, Velliya Nadar knew how to make arrack. And he made a lot of profits. He bought several shops at auction and grew rich. It was at this time that the Dutch government sold Porayar, Tranquebar and its other possessions to the British people, including this, Company's Garden.'

I asked how the name had arisen.

'This place was formerly an arsenal, used by the Danish people.' Like many others, he used the words Dutch and Danish synonymously. 'Then it passed to the British and it was the Tanjore Collector who sold this place to Velliya Nadar. Ever since it has been known as Company's Garden. I think that the name is from your East India Company.

'Velliya Nadar had two sons. The eldest was Thavasumuthu Nadar. This son was also a very clever man, and he built up his father's business. In his time he established several distilleries which supplied arrack to various districts across south India. He also purchased lands, to the extent of about six thousand acres in various villages.'

A power cut interrupted him. The single fluorescent tube above the bed was extinguished and the fan revolved into immobility. After a moment he got up and went to open the lower casement. The window faced east towards the sea and a touch of breeze reached Porayar, a kilometre inland.

'Thavasumuthu had three sons, namely R. Ratnasamy, Vellaithambi and Gurusamy. He became eminent. It was he who founded

126

Thavasumuthu Nadar Higher Secondary School, here in Porayar, some hundred and twenty years back. For his service to the community, the British government conferred on him the title Rao Bahadur. During this period British governors used to come and stay in our seaside bungalow as guests. During my father Gurusamy Nadar's period Cochin Highness stayed in said bungalow as a guest.'

The servant came in with a thermos of coffee, a packet of biscuits, and a pink plastic bag, the contents of which did not meet approval. He was sent back to the shop.

'My apologies. We are not in the habit of serving cake here. I can remember having tea with British people. There was a visit to the Carltons in Madras, shortly before the Second Great War. Carlton you know was a district magistrate, promoted to the collectorship at Tanjore and hence to the government at Madras. His wife made a most wonderful cake.'

He stretched, scratched his shoulder and took up the story again. His generation had seen the splintering of his grandfather's estate. 'The sons of Ratnasamy, Vellaithambi and Gurusamy picked a quarrel and filed a partition suit in the High Court at Madras. The court appointed Messrs Fraser & Ross – that was the name, Fraser & Ross C.A., chartered accountants – as receivers. Later on all the properties were divided, meats and bones, by the High Court.'

I asked what was the cause of the quarrel.

'Oh, the usual thing here. Inheritance. The eldest of the cousins refused to pay money to the other heirs. So, as I say, it was all divided, meats and bones. The business remaining was converted into a limited company under the name of The Nadar Distilleries Ltd. During this period the Governor of Madras Lord Goschen visited Tranquebar and stayed in our seaside bungalow for a day or so.'

Independence had dealt the final blow. 'The Congress Party came into power and introduced prohibition. As a result of this we had to close down our distilleries.'

'Did you receive compensation?'

'No compensation was paid to us. No compensation was paid to us. You may write that down.'

He returned to his notes. 'So, uh, income from the properties remaining are not adequate, not adequate. We had distilleries at

127

Madurai, Thirunelveli, Cochin, many places; even at Jaipur and in Orissa province. And now the whole family is in distress.'

He went on, reading carefully. 'We were all along loyal to the British Government. And the British were very helpful to us. So what I would say now is, if it is possible for you, please help me by getting sole agency for any British product to India or any benefit from the British government. For such acts I will be ever grateful.'

At last the servant returned, this time with a bag of very sweet cakes coated in green icing. I had to explain that I was a person of little influence in England.

T.G. said that he had an English cousin somewhere. One of Rao Bahadur's sons had studied in Reading and married an Englishwoman. 'He tried to return home during the war, but could not get a passage. We heard that he went mad in the London Blitz. He died, and his wife sold up his property here. I am told there is a daughter, Sita, still alive.'

His talk circled back to the subject of the family's decline. Not only had the distillery business been killed by prohibition, but the family estates had been affected by land reforms. This battle he was still fighting. 'What do the land reforms mean? Communists are giving a lot of trouble. The tenants are not paying us the scheduled amount but we cannot remove the tenants. And for this same reason we cannot sell our properties. So our income is reduced by a considerable extent. We are in the hands of these political fellows.'

Yet on the wall I saw that he had put up a couple of small photographs of himself with Tamil Nadu politicians, a record of handshakes and garlanding at official functions. He was not deprived of all power or resources. He had recently set up a rice mill in the Company's Garden compound, and was awaiting the licence for a second mill to make groundnut oil. According to Dr Chandrasekaran, his daughter was very rich, her husband the proprietor of a Tamil tabloid, the *Daily Thanti*, a copy of which lay discarded by the lawyer on the bed. In addition, T. G. Ratnasamy was president of the Nadar sangam, or caste association, which had been founded by Rao Bahadur early in the century. The caste associations worked towards the improvement in status of a caste as a whole, where this was not possible for individuals. In a century they had shown that, even in the rigidly stratified society of the south, upliftment could be achieved by organ-isation, by establishing schools and funding scholarships. Their leaders had influence. Of the several lakhs of people in the Nadar caste, five thousand attended the sangam's annual conference at Madurai, to which state and sometimes national politicians were attracted as speakers.

T. G. Ratnasamy was leaving shortly for the week of celebrations that would follow the wedding of his grandson in Thirunelveli. He showed me the invitation on thick gold-rimmed card. There would be five hundred guests. When he returned he would send someone to invite us to dinner.

'Do you like biryani?' He made meat-eating sound a sensual plea-sure. At times a man could revel in low caste, and leave the brahmins to their curd and dahls.

19

The father of the Muslim girls came home from Singapore. I surprised him in his house, following Tom as he trotted in after Jebin and Marhin. He was sitting on the edge of the brass bed, cooling off with a red towel over his head. Indians had a characteristic way with pieces of cloth, using them to answer nuances of mood or temperature, draping them round head or neck or over the shoulder with careless movements as the moment suggested. Even when men stood to talk on the street you might see them unconsciously smooth, fold and rearrange the flapping lengths of cotton they wore.

I knew Shahabudeen's face already from the photograph that hung in the hall. This photograph had been taken some years before. Shot from a low angle, it made him a matinée idol, all chiselled features and shadowy eyes. It must have been taken around the time of his marriage, for he wears the same sharp suit in the wedding photographs, tailored in Singapore and chosen to match the sari he had bought for Yasmin; the colourist at the photo studio had shaded their clothes violet but Yasmin kept the original sari stored in a trunk under the bed, bronze satin, embroidered and sequined.

His hair had greyed and receded since the photo, and his face had hollowed, the fine structure and long eyes showing the source of Jebin's Ancient Egyptian profile. He was tall, ascetically thin. His dignity was unimpaired by the towel, which he took from his head and slung round his neck.

The whole family came with us that evening when we walked to the beach and we stayed late, past the quick sunset. Shahabudeen strode ahead at the edge of the waves. Jebin ran to catch him up and he paused and they stooped to play at collecting mussels in the sand. Yasmin rid herself of her fardtha – there was no one to see her so far down the beach – and ran to join them. She began to gather mussels in earnest, wading in a few inches of water, her fingers swiftly scooping little troughs behind each wave.

Some way back, little Marhin sat on a log from a catamaran. She had put on her mother's robe and sat hunched before the wind that came off the sea, the white fabric parachuting out behind her.

Shahabudeen imposed formality on the household of women, so that I was given a chair whenever I entered, and treated with solicitous courtesy. He saw to it that at the Muslim festival of Muhurram one of the girls brought round to me a dish of special sweet rice. Next day he inquired how I had liked it and announced that he had prepared it for me himself, but had to refer to Yasmin to name the ingredients and thus guiltlessly revealed that his role had been no more than supervisory.

He had been born in Malacca, in 1942 when Malaya was under Japanese occupation, his only papers a birth certificate issued by the Japanese. His parents, as Indian citizens, had been required to leave Malaya following the war, and he had grown up in Nagapattinam. They had lived in a large house, his father being an educated man, a translator among other things, and rising to local importance. He told me of places I should see at Nagapattinam, and the stories associated with them, twisting, disconnected tales of Dutch treasure, of a tunnel that ran to the palace at Tanjore, of a stolen Buddha's head of solid gold.

He had once made a journey to Goa and it had impressed him. It was beautiful and historical, the girls wore skirts and the body of Saint Francis Xavier lay mummified in a golden basilica. It appealed to the aesthetic, the flashy, and the religious in his nature. Singapore he found too modern. Modern India he despised for its ugly monuments. On the outskirts of Karikal stood a statue of a famous Tamil politician, a crude and ill-proportioned concrete figure. When our bus passed, his nose wrinkled with the same disgust he expressed at the smell of pork frying in Chinese restaurants in Singapore. 'The British built fine memorials. So many of them, each and everywhere, and they will last for centuries. Why is it that the Indians cannot do as well? Indians, whose sculpture was once so very fine?'

He was a trader of a kind. He liked to say he dealt in antiques. I

131

asked what sort. He said stamps, coins, et cetera: his business was multifarious. From the top of a wardrobe he took down a white cotton shopping bag, and unwrapped the tissue paper from a dozen miniature glass vases. They were tawdry things four inches high, decorated with sprigs of roses. He handled them fastidiously and did not say if they were to his taste. 'I carried these on the airplane from Singapore. They are made in Japan. They will sell very well here.'

He had a dealer in mind at Nagore. And he had other contacts, at Nagapattinam, at the foreign market in Karikal, and further afield at Tanjore and Trichinopoly. 'The profits are good on glassware because it is so breakable. Very few people risk to carry it. Twenty-five times cost price.'

A dozen little glass vases was a tiny trade but it was as much as the local market for luxuries could support. Other goods he had brought back from Singapore had been sold in Madras immediately on arrival: small electronic things, calculators and radios; though these were more expensive items he said they yielded a smaller percentage profit. It was picking a living, one man selling little more than he could carry on board a plane. He had been travelling to and from Singapore a couple of times a year for twenty years. Formerly he had made the journey by ship, on the M.V. *Chidambaram*, the same ageing Shipping Corporation of India liner on which I had first come to India, and reckoning back, Shaha thought that he had made the same passage in 1981. The coincidence was significant for him, though we could not have met since he had travelled deep below decks in the third-class berths which the agents refused to sell to Europeans.

Bhanu had hinted of financial worries: a run of bad luck, a dishonest partner, a suitcase that went missing between Singapore and Madras. Local prices were so low that even a trickle of foreign earnings would be enough just to feed the family. But they needed capital. They wanted to live at Nagapattinam but rented accommodation was scarce since the oil and gas field had been opened nearby. To buy a house they needed two and a half lakhs of rupees. Then Bhanu was of marriageable age and Shirin was approaching it. Another two lakhs were needed for each dowry. Shaha looked for a big deal.

Hope rested in twenty-seven copper coins from Sarawak, and

possibly in my assistance. A numismatic directory illustrated a similar Sarawak coin, Arabic lettering on one face and the outline of a badger on the other, and identified it as an early token issued by Rajah Brooke, valued at four hundred US dollars. The coins Shaha possessed might then have been worth a good couple of lakhs.

'There is a Mr C. N. Desai, a coin dealer of Gujarat. I sent him a letter some time back and he expressed interest. But now I have received a second correspondence from him. Please read it.'

Mr Desai's first letter was very positive. His second curtly rejected an offer of sixteen of the coins for three thousand rupees apiece, making the numismatic distinction that they were technically tokens, issued without monetary value, to which his dealing did not extend.

'How do you understand this?'

I asked if he thought it was a ploy.

'But Mr Desai is an honourable man. He is well known. No, I think I shall send him some of the coins and tell him to name his own price.'

I thought his suggestion either naïve or desperate. I looked again at the coins. Perhaps they were too good to be true, a little too uniformly worn.

Two weeks later an English numismatist turned up at Tranquebar. I met him outside the Indian Bank, a GP from Croydon trailing a pair of Tamil street urchins. He appeared like some kind of Father Christmas, a burly man with matted white hair, hot, smiling and open handed.

I invited him round and introduced him to Shaha. The Muslim sat in silence as he drank two cups of tea and told me how he came to be at Tranquebar. He had flown to Bombay initially for a numismatic conference and a short holiday. At Bombay he was flattered to be invited to lecture at Calcutta, where he had been put up by the Victoria Memorial Museum. He was enthusiastic about Calcutta: there was a general strike while he was there and he saw people playing cricket on the main thoroughfares. He had then come south, to Madurai. He met the urchins, bright boys who made a living off the tourists at the temple and spoke snippets of four European languages, and discovered they had never seen the sea. It was only then that he had thought of Tranquebar. He knew about the place because of its Danish colonial coins, the early ones being collectors' curiosities, each issue bearing the name of a Danish ship.

The urchins fidgeted while he talked. They were evidently disappointed. The beach full of fishermen and the room they had been given at the Spiritual Centre were hardly what they expected of travel with a Westerner. The numismatist asked if there was a proper resort on the Coromandel Coast. Somewhere with a funfair.

Before his expansiveness Shaha had retracted into inscrutability. He brought out a slim envelope of folded white paper and spread the coins before us on the table.

'So what have we here?'

Shaha showed him the directory entry.

'Sarawak, not my field. Interesting, though, to see the badger of the White Rajas. I never thought before of the connection: Brooke, brock, and brock you know an old word for badger. But it's really not my field. My speciality is the native Indian coinage. I really hoped I might come across some Akbar coins. Do you see any of those?'

Shaha's expression was taut. 'Sir, you know this directory, do you not?'

'Oh, very reliable, Yeoman. But this edition's a few years old. The values could have risen since.'

'And do you know Mr C. N. Desai of Gujarat?'

'No. I'm afraid we've never met.'

'You have heard his name?'

'To be quite honest, no.'

The numismatist recommended an auction house in London. Shaha pressed me to take some of the coins there on my return. (Sadly, neither Phillips, Glendinning nor Spink's were to be persuaded of their authenticity.)

Whatever Shaha's business worries, there did not seem to be much he could do about them. For the couple of months he stayed at Tranquebar, he left his deals to germinate. He read a newspaper occasionally and comments passed across from his veranda to Wilson's. Once I went in to find him reading from a plastic-covered notebook, densely handwritten. Its subject was the lives of Muslim saints and he had copied out the text himself from a book that belonged to a friend. Another day he borrowed a book of mine, a guide to Indian birds. He brought it back a few hours later. 'This is a very good book. I have shot forty-two of these species of birds.'

But he had sold his gun in December, an old rifle, for six hundred rupees.

For a long time we planned an expedition to Nagapattinam. We would combine the trip with a visit to the dealer he had mentioned at Nagore. But one day I put it off and the next Shaha had a sudden appointment. It was a couple of weeks before we finally went up to the bus stand. Shaha put on a pressed white shirt to go into town and pinched the fold in his outer dhoti ruler-straight before the mirror.

As we left a beggar came through the gate. He came each morning, a smooth-faced young man in a green turban, and stopped before 16A. He beat a tambourine and wailed a brief verse, paused a minute and then passed on. I had never seen them give him money but someone must have done. Shaha said he did the rounds of the Muslim homes of Tranquebar and Porayar each day. 'That is a very lazy man.'

At the bus stand we waited an hour and a quarter. When a bus did come for Karikal and Nagapattinam it was overflowing.

'Too much a crush.' Shaha scanned the bodies hanging out the doors. 'Let us try again another day.' We strolled home, he all the time carrying the fragile bag of Singapore glassware.

A week later we were again at the bus stand, bound for the durga of a local saint on the second anniversary of his death. The saint had lived at the mosque for twenty-five years and was well known in the Nagapattinam district; Shaha expected that we would even meet his friend Subramanian, the brahmin Customs Superintendent, among the devotees.

Shaha had visited the saint over a period of ten years. He had asked him directly for advice. He believed the saint had great power, an intermediary between himself and God who was as necessary, he said, as a transformer on an electrical circuit: connect an ordinary man directly to God and he would blow. One time he had gone to the saint and asked if he should take a second wife. The answer had been immediate: how could he, a poor man who had nothing, take in another woman? So Shaha had stuck with one wife and four

135

daughters. He saw now that it would have been too great a gamble to expect only sons from a second marriage.

We got on the bus beside an elderly Muslim, hunched like a mantis, who was the Arabic teacher from the mosque school. When we were already approaching Karikal he mentioned that he had attended the durga on the previous evening. Shaha and I were a day late.

'So it goes,' said Shaha.

In Nagapattinam then we simply made the rounds. A coffee by the bus stand, and then a swift walk to the centre of town, the road dark, the tarmac certain underfoot, the dust soft and treacherous when the traffic pushed us off course and we had to grope back to the road wary of potholes and open drains. Under one of the scattered streetlamps sat a palmist, under the next an astrologer with a green parakeet in a cage. The bird was trained to pick out paper predictions from a box.

I asked Shaha if he believed in astrology.

'Fifty per cent.'

'How's that?'

'For me, the bad things come as predicted. The good things, never. But that astrologer with the parrot is no use. Do not trust a parrot.'

The market area was bright with the fluorescent lights of open shops and stalls, which obliterated the stars but did not reveal the squalor on the ground, giving the streets a glamour they would have lacked by day. We shopped, bought chappati flour and a special kind of sweet, and checked the winning numbers of the lotteries for Yasmin's mother. There was a shop selling bits of metal. Before it lay crates heaped with scrap, lockless keys and loose nuts. Shaha picked through with long fingers, eyes narrowed. He had found coins before in places like this.

We had a more leisurely coffee at the watchmaker's. The Hindu who ran the shop was an old friend and colleague. He had accompanied Shaha on his journey to Goa, a thousand miles by train to meet dealers in clocks and coins. He was a dark Tamil, not thin but light in his movements as if he was. The shop was a narrow room up a few steep steps from the street. We sat on wooden stools lined up against the wall, beneath five pendulum clocks that moved almost in unison, so close to the counter that the coffee boy could not squeeze by and we must pass a cup along to the old Hindu astrologer who had his place at the end. Shaha told me this man was a good and authentic astrologer. The ritual ash smeared across his forehead made him look like a ghost.

The watchmaker sat behind the counter in a kind of booth enclosed by glass panels in an attempt to keep out the dust. White paper was laid beneath the glass tabletop, and pressed there beneath the delicate tools was a minuscule, fingernail image of Ganesh, the pot-bellied and elephant-headed deity of enterprise. A second Ganesh in brass sat on the counter, no larger than the lime placed in offering before it. In an hour the watchmaker did perhaps five minutes' work, angling his metal lamp and his magnifying glass low over the table and meticulously cleaning cogs held with tweezers. There was no more urgency to his business than there was backlog, and the glass display case by the steps to the street contained at most half a dozen old watches and as many alarm clocks. He too picked at his living, day by day. They lived like birds, he and Shaha. And for him there was the threat of digital competition, the high-tech watches from the Far East that made his skills redundant.

Shaha asked me if there was a good market for organs in England. 'Organs?'

'Church organs. Second-hand.' Apparently Reverend Williams at the CSI church had one to sell. 'It is very fine, two hundred years old. People will pay much for such old things. It is British-made, from the city of Derby, seven pipes, bellows type, condition a little worn.'

20

In the fields by the Mission Garden, the green brilliance of the samba
rice had dulled, that before had thrown the mango grove into
dark relief against the open land. At the far edge of the grove a
path ran through a field to a roughly shaped tank. Beyond the tank,
by walking at the edge of squares of rice, a temple could be
reached. It was a small country temple and it was full of squirrels.
The festival images stored in the colonnade within its walls were
battered as old fairground horses: a trunkless Ganesh, the peacock of Sarasvati with rivets through its mirrored tail, bleared with
dust.

At the tank, a woman bathed. She had tied one end of her indigo
sari beneath her shoulders and the remaining loose yards of fabric,
buoyed up by trapped air, billowed about her on the olive-brown
water. She raised an arm to spread her hair for washing.

She had only a small clearing to bathe in since most of the surface
was covered with waterlilies. Three boys had plucked some of the
huge pink flowers and made chains of them, breaking the succulent
stems into sections that were held together only by the stringy outer
threads, and bending them round. A bird swooped from the mast
tree where they sat on the bank, jet black with a forked tail. A
green parakeet followed. The Indian birds were elegantly oriental,
iridescent, long tailed, but raucous. The softest notes were those of
a cuckoo, indolent as the movement of the woman in the water. I
saw three species of kingfisher come to the tank: the small common
kingfisher that is so shy in Europe, a big and flashy pied bird and
another that had a white chest and a streak of the characteristic blue
across the back of its wings. Fishing, they would hover first, bill
down, tail down, body bent at an acute angle, then shoot vertically
right into the water and up again. Seen in a moment of inaction, on
a branch or on a telegraph wire over an irrigation ditch, kingfishers

were stocky, wedge-shaped birds: that bullet flight required instant power.

A dirt road passed on the other side of the temple, where its gate opened on to a kind of square before the brahmins' houses. The road ran to the village of Erukkattanchery, then forked to either side of the compound of another, larger temple and broke into rambling streets. It was hard to gauge the size of these inland villages, built at random, spread across flat ground where there was no vantage point to reveal their extent. Hidden away at Erukkattanchery were a number of prosperous-looking houses, modern concrete villas of two storeys with iron balconies and painted walls around their gardens.

The postmaster said that the village had a population of five thousand.

'The village receives one postal delivery a day, letters and money orders, and each day the postbox collects fifty or sixty envelopes.'

'So you are not too busy?'

He sat on the platform that raised his veranda above the dust of the street, back to a wooden column, legs loosely crossed. The sleeves of his white shirt were neatly folded up to the elbow, above his silver watch.

'There are in addition the telegram communications, which require immediate attention and delivery. Only today the telegraph line through Porayar is down. Telegrams now are coming only to Mayuram.'

'You have a lovely post office here.'

'Yes indeed. This post office reached the finals of the Clean Post Office competition, Madras Circle, in 1975.'

On the sign at the office entrance, beneath the low palm-thatch awning, the red paint was fresh. The finish on the postbox, to one side of the veranda, was equally slick, the single collection time minutely hand lettered. The office itself took up the other half of the veranda, enclosed by a slatted partition. On the polished wooden desk, a pen, a pencil, a stamp pad and a couple of rubber stamps were symmetrically arranged. Above the desk hung the competition certificate; further along the white wall, a calendar, and a group photograph of the staff at an earlier date. The postmaster pointed out his father at the centre of the picture, postmaster before him.

Behind the heavy doors encrusted with chrome yellow gods was the family home. The post office was the family business, passed on to the eldest son. A younger brother was a life insurance salesman and it was his company's calendar that hung in the office. Both brothers resembled their father as he had been in mid-life, relaxed, well fleshed, with thin moustaches and oiled hair.

In the villages people were known better by occupation than by name. My neighbours referred to Wilson as the headmaster, to Sheikh Allauddin as the houseowner (in Indian usage the word 'landlord' being more equivalent to the British 'landowner'). It was a static society in which the position of each member was clearly labelled. The postmaster need be only that; there was no differentiation between public and private identity, office and home, work and leisure. His self-assurance, inherited with his title, could be complete.

A short way beyond the Mission Garden, towards Mayuram, was the parkland leading down to the river where the ruins of Smith's house stood. The place was called Ohruga Mangalam, the name itself meaning the mango grove. The trees were huge and old, tamarinds as well as mangoes, both spreading shade trees with hard dark leaves.

The scattered shrines and images of an old temple shared the park, the main building close to the river upstream of Smith's house but hidden from view by clumps of cashews that were low and billowing like green cumulus. The well at the temple had fresh kolam designs painted on its concrete surround. Just by stood an ungainly pottery horse, heavy with ritual trappings and held by stumpy Hindu figures that reached only to its withers. Though the sanctuary seemed derelict the small lingam before it was anointed with oil and sandal paste.

The temple at the centre of the hamlet of Ohruga Mangalam was obviously better used, with new paint caked over the old layers on its walls. Before the temple was a steep-sided tank. The water was muddy, thick with weed and teeming with small fish and frogs that the children caught. Opposite, on the step of a sentry-box shrine, sat a holy man with a sun-blackened body and a long white beard. At the temple a conch was blown, the sound running smooth against the caw of crows. It was the temple of Mariamman, the goddess who controlled smallpox, chickenpox, typhoid and cholera.

The next village along the road was Thirukaddiyar, where the temple housed a deity known as the Lord Controller of Time. There was a story that once a devout youth called Markandeya came to pray there. Markandeya was sixteen and he had been allotted only sixteen years of life. He prayed for an extension and the god protected him. He embraced the god and became merged with him so that when the Lord Yama, the lord of death, came to him, he had to throw his noose round both boy and god in order to pull him to the underworld. But the Lord Shiva, more powerful than the others, appeared and cried, 'This is my pure devotee. He no one can destroy.' Markandeya was taken by Shiva into eternal life, beyond the cycle of death and rebirth.

'How lucky it is for the priests in this village that this was the place where Markandeya prayed.' I talked with a smiling brahmin from Madras. He had come, with fifty or sixty other members of his family, to mark the approach of his sister's sixtieth birthday. The event was reckoned so important that the entire extended family had gathered from Madras and further afield and had rented a house at Thirukaddi-yur for twenty-four hours. 'This day, you must know, was decreed by my sister's astrologers to be propitious for the celebration of a puja for the prolongation of her life. The puja must be made at this very temple, before this very god; for the Hindu world is multifarious and possesses a god for each job and each duty.'

Though dusty and unadorned, the temple was known to be very rich. It attracted more devotees, more wealthy and eminent brah-mins, than many architecturally finer temples. For them, its priests laid on elaborate ceremonies. I watched with the family as five priests chanted and burnt camphor in the dark hall before the sanctuary of the god, the flames leaping up before soot-blackened columns. The chant extended, rose and faded. In its diminuendo rose the sound of the chant in the neighbouring shrine, where another ceremony was simultaneously in progress. When it came to an end, the priests led the family out into the light, to the well where each one of them

141

poured sacred water over the yellow-garlanded heads of the old woman and her husband. The passage from shade to light was dramatic, a transformation taking place between one pillar and the next as the procession moved from the hall into the courtyard: the men in fine white cotton, the women in silk saris of peacock shades, woven with bands of gold thread.

The rival ceremony was more solemn, a single grey-haired man seated before the priests at a shrine to the side of the sanctuary, behind him only a couple of companions and the temple musicians. Three or four policemen skulked in the shadows of the surrounding colonnade, rural policemen in village-tailored khaki. We talked as the chants wore on. They were Porayar police detailed to VIP duty. The devotee was no less than a high court judge at Madras.

The temple did unending trade. Each day must see someone reaching sixty. I went by it often. Though it lay back from the road as you approached the village, it showed before the low village houses, the four great pyramidal gateways jutting above the skyline of palms. The view was a typical one in the region. The gateways, known as gopuras, are the grandest features of south Indian temples: wedge shaped, rising in decreasing tiers to a narrow barrelled roof, the whole outline blurred with massed sculpture and the roof topped by a line of bulbous finials and ending in curling scallops stuffed with gods.

A line of old banyans ran along the road out from the village, to a bridge where there was a bathing place with steps down to the river. Women would pass, returning from the ghat. They padded by wearing the wet saris they had washed as they bathed and their hair hung in damp tails down their backs. I sometimes took a track from there out through the fields towards Tillially. The people who worked in the fields despaired of the harvest. In most places the rice had received only the rains that year and no irrigation from the Cauvery. They shook their heads in resignation and spoke of the lack of water from the Mettur dam.

I talked with an old man who was turning rice straw to dry. He looked like an old soldier and had a few curt words of English. 'Cultivating, no use. Ten years here, no water. Rainwater only.' Others said five years, others two. The plain facts were that the year's first harvest had been lost already, and the second, the samba, promised nothing. The rice would not fatten, would yield little more than its straw, which was used for cattle fodder.

The old man had brought his two cows to graze beside him as he worked. He had a white stubble on his chin and wore a rough green turban to shade his head from the sun. He said how the villagers had been affected. The areas closest to the sea had been worst hit. In the last few years they had not even planted rice on the two kilometres of land between the Thirukaddiyur road and the shore. He was lucky that his fields were on this side. There, people had been forced to sell up, for low prices, and live on in their villages without income. They went to the moneylenders and they sought work in other men's fields at harvest time – but there was little enough of that: only a few days in a year, and then sometimes four workers would share a single job. Some men had left their families behind and gone to Kerala to the tea plantations.

Three fishing women passed by on the track in single file, baskets of fish on their heads. They walked erect, in slow procession, their saris sombre shades of green and claret. The farmer watched their straight backs as they turned by some trees. 'They are very poor people,' he said. They were walking all the way to Tillially, and if their fish was not sold there they would walk on. The river fishing also had declined, and some of their men too had had to go down the coast or across to Kerala.

I followed the route he had indicated, along the uneven raised paths beside futile irrigation channels. Soon I overtook the fishing women. Their faces carried the salty rigour of the beach into the deceptive green softness inland. In Tranquebar everyone I met spoke of someone else as being very poor. It was hard to know which group was the poorest. A farmer waited for the next harvest. A fisherman could at least hope for a catch each day.

No rice had been planted that year on the land before the rivermouth at Tranquebar. The ground had acquired a white crust of salt. It was drained of moisture, its colours neutralised. The only vibrance left in that landscape was in the birds, white egrets and blue-green bee-eaters. The still grey water of the old port was distinguished from the grey mudbanks chiefly by its sheen. In the distance, along the sand-strip between the lagoon and the sea, the casuarinas stood like tired pines, their limp needles bluish as trees in a faded watercolour.

There was a hamlet on the other side of the rivermouth, hidden from the road by scrub. In this densely populated region such hamlets were common, sometimes no more than four or five houses clustered along a path in the fields, with a few trees for shade. This one was home to about a hundred people.

Vijay Kumar had been born there. He was now in his twenties, tall for a Tamil, pleasant looking, quietly spoken. Proximity to Tranquebar had brought him a Catholic education though his family was Hindu. He had gone to St Joseph's junior school, up the road by the Catholic church. Later he had gained a B.A. in history. He was currently doing an M.A. by correspondence course and hoped to go on to a B.Ed. The impressive curriculum vitae was not unusual. The woman who sold me bantam eggs from her home in Queen Street had a master's degree. Like other unemployed graduates, Vijay continued to qualify himself in the absence of anything better to do. He was also studying catechism, for conversion to Christianity. The little cloth shop he had opened in the row by the bus stand had few customers and brought in barely three hundred rupees a month.

Vijay's family lived in a large turquoise-painted hut at the edge of the hamlet. His aunt and uncle had lived next door until their kerosene stove set fire to their house. Vijay had closed the shop to help them rebuild. In three days they had the framework up, the raised mud floor almost to full height, the mud walls halfway. The work would be finished within a week. The materials had cost around two thousand rupees: thin red bricks for the low walls, wooden struts, bamboo rafters for the long pitched roof, dried palm leaves to be woven into thatch, coir rope to tie the thatch sheets to the bamboos.

By the end of January, the channel that had cut through the beach south of the fort, between the old port and the sea, was dry sand. Presumably if water had come down the Cauvery as in the past, it would not have dried at least until the hot weather. But it was possible now to walk directly on from the Tranquebar beach, beyond the last of the catamarans, to the line of casuarinas.

When Regina Mary went home at the end of each afternoon, I took Tom to the beach. Often we met ASR, the retired pastor, who set off at the same time for his daily visit to his wife's grave. Flora Rajendram had died in January or February of the previous year, and when her anniversary came up a granite headstone was erected in the New Cemetery outside the old town wall. Perhaps this also marked the end of a period of mourning, since after that day we met him less often. We even found him down on the beach himself, led by his granddaughter, though he had said that the sea airs were not good for his arthritic bones.

Sometimes we went into the fort, up the ramp to the battlements where there was clear space for Tom to run in and steps for him to climb. Few others came there, only women and girls who took water from the well on its walls. The sea had a different aspect when you looked down from the parapet. It flattened and seemed a piece of fabric in which individual waves were woven together. In oblique light it could be like shot silk, smoky coloured, the sun catching the wave crests like rough threads.

BEWARE GODS,
REMEMBER MAN

21

A monument to Rao Bahadur Nadar stood on the main road opposite the Landgate. It came into view as you walked up King Street, set in the distance within the frame of the Danish arch, a slim obelisk Indianised by a lotus-bud finial. The monument had been erected in 1926 at the apex of the Nadar fortunes. The foundation stone had been laid, in a formal ceremony, by Mr J. A. Thorne, the British Additional District Magistrate at Tanjore.

In 1982, the Town Rationalist Forum had put up, between the obelisk and the bus shelter, a black stone tablet in a concrete slab. The tablet was engraved in Tamil and English.

ADVICES OF PERIYAR

No god! No god!
No god exist at all!!!
Creator of god is a fool!
Propagator of god is a scoundrel!!
Believer of god is a barbarian!!!
Relinquish god! Remind man!!

I was waiting for a bus. It was early afternoon and the shelter gave airless shade. The phrases on the tablet hung in the heat like a spell, as flies clustered on something rotten among the filth on the floor. Some fishing women were squatting beside baskets loaded with fish. The skin on their narrow backs, exposed under rose and turquoise saris, was cracked like dry leather. The woman closest to me – who looked old though Regina Mary could no doubt have told me she was only forty – stretched out one leg before her and rubbed it as if it had no feeling. The leg was blistered and swollen from the ankle up. Another woman did something I often observed: she pulled out from her waist the tucked corner of her sari where she kept her money knotted, counted out a fistful of ten-paise coins that could barely have amounted to two rupees, then carefully laid them in a roll, folded them round with the cloth and tucked them in again.

What good were gods to them? Was that what Periyar was saying? There was an argument that without their gods, their lives would be unbearable. There was another that without the gods, change would be possible.

I found the headmaster of the TELC teacher training college beside me. I asked what people had thought when the Rationalists put up their monument.

'It is a public place. Each man may express his opinion.'

'But did it make anyone angry?'

'Certainly, some do not like it. But to many here these are golden words.'

'And do you agree with them?'

'How can I, being a Christian?' But he added, 'I must tell you that Periyar was not speaking of Christianity. Nor of the Muslim religion either. He was speaking of Hinduism. He criticised the *Ramayana* and the *Mahabharata*. He attacked caste observance. Whatever else you may say of him, of one thing there is no doubt, that he is one of our greatest social reformers. Poor people, the adidravida, gave him their weight in sugar.'

The headmaster went on to say that before his death at the famous Christian hospital in Vellore, Periyar had turned to Christianity.

'This is not generally known, and there are many who would not like it to be said. But he spoke with the doctors and nurses, and we have their words on it.'

Periyar the atheist had been pretty much deified since his death in 1973. Periyar was an early member of the Indian National Congress, but even before Independence he had become diverted from national to Tamil politics. In 1925 he had founded the Self-Respect Movement, preaching a populist combination of rationalism, socialism and Tamil nationalism. The basis, and the force, of the Movement came from the outrage he expressed at brahminism, caste and Hinduism, and the sacred licence these gave to inequality.

At that time the brahmins were visibly the élite of Tamil Nadu, distinguished by their fair skin and etched Aryan features from the mass of the darker Tamils. Brahmins ran the temples, which had always given them control of vast wealth and tracts of land, and since they were traditionally the most educated class, they also made up the majority of the administrators, judges and doctors in the region. Tamil resentment took shape in the mood of self-discovery that accompanied the struggle against the British. Under Periyar's leadership, the new Dravidian awareness recognised the Tamil identity as that of the original inhabitants of the subcontinent who had been displaced, way back in history, by the influx of the Aryans. At its extreme, it perceived in brahmin power another and earlier form of colonialism, espoused ideas of autonomy from Delhi, and dreamt of a return to Chola glory. More simply, it gave confidence to the lower castes – thus the assertiveness now given to the term adidravida, used to describe the Tamil untouchable.

Periyar's ideas found political expression after Independence in the DMK party. Campaigning with a grass-roots energy, the DMK first came to power in Tamil Nadu in 1967 and immediately enforced a radical programme of levelling. Tamil Nadu saw the reservation of jobs and college places for people of lower castes long before this was applied in the rest of India, also the reform of temple administration and the redistribution of temple lands. The DMK remained in government until it was dismissed by Indira Gandhi in the 1976 State of Emergency, to be re-elected in 1988. There had been time for its policies to have clear results, including a decline of brahmin and temple power, and an exodus of educated brahmin youth seeking qualifications and employment elsewhere in India or abroad.

Even so, Tamil Nadu was still one of the most conservative states in India as far as caste was concerned. Reservations, appointments and college places were irrelevant for most members of the lowest castes, for the peasants and the uneducated – sometimes peasants may even have lost out by the measures, as the temple may have been a more benevolent landowner than a private individual. In the villages, tradition was stronger than contemporary politics. Rigid caste observance still applied, between the plethora of different castes and sub-castes that varied from one district to the next.

I saw this in action only through my contact with the Christians.

151

There was a young TELC priest who went to live in a village inland from Tranquebar. He was adidravida himself and the Lutheran church was in the adidravida part of the village, but he could find a house to rent only in a caste district. All had gone satisfactorily for a while, until his neighbours sent a deputation to ask him to move. With due politeness they announced that he they could accept, on account of his position and education, but his visitors polluted the street. From the Tamil viewpoint, the more remarkable aspect of this story may have been that the education of the pastor had at first succeeded in winning a small degree of flexibility from the old system.

22

A young German woman called Helga Fritz ran a TELC orphanage at Porayar. She was of the modern school, more aid worker than missionary, social reform being indivisible from the rest of her work. She was a Western liberal, her sympathies with the underprivileged, women and those of low caste.

There were contradictions in her position. She was embarrassed to be a white woman managing Indians. She called herself simply a 'co-worker' and her objective when she finished her contract was to have no replacement from Europe but to leave local women in charge. Before Independence white woman missionaries wore cotton dresses and ankle socks. In the 1950s many put on saris. Helga learnt to wear a sari soon after she arrived at Porayar, in an attempt to close the gap between herself and the Indians. Then for a time she moved completely into Western dress, as if to clarify her differ-ence. She had tried Punjabi dress, the long tunic and trousers of north India which it is easy for Western women to wear. After two years she had ended up back in Western dress but putting on a sari for formal occasions.

She was wearing a sari when I met her first at a village wedding. It was a snobbish affair. The bride was from a prominent Lutheran family and the groom was managing director of a building firm in Pudukottai, his status announced in print on the invitations. All the leading members of the TELC community put in an appearance, plus Sheikh Allauddin's uncle, the lone Muslim, and in the course of the interminable reception most of them had to get up on a dais beside the couple and say something or other. Helga had been the bride's employer. Her speech was brief and she told me after that she had upset her church superiors by failing to refer to the orphanage with sufficient formality.

Her belief in equality was fundamental to her religion and required itself to be seen in directness of relationships. But she found engrained in her Indian co-workers a sense of hierarchy and an old-fashioned propriety close to that of the colonial missionaries from whom she wished to distance herself. They liked to address her by her title (as Regina Mary stubbornly refused to call me anything but Madam, however many times I asked her). They thought it right that a lesson should be halted and an entire class stand if she looked into one of the orphanage classrooms. They were authoritarian and they were paternalistic towards the uneducated, whom they tended to regard as unfortunate inferiors. For all the conscientious charity of their Christianity, their judgments were still founded in caste. So Helga worked towards incompatible ends: she worked to enable the establishment to take on a more Indian identity, and she worked to bring to it her foreign egalitarianism.

We had lunch with her where she lived, in a high-ceilinged room. The long veranda where we sat afterwards had white columns and morning glory covered the trellis between them. For Helga, a touch of guilt attached to its colonial beauty. While she felt she should have been able to work in the Calcutta slums, she admitted that there were times when she needed this spaciousness and calm. Her rooms were airy with the sea breeze. Her bedroom on the floor above caught that breeze even in summer. It looked out across an open stretch of pasture towards the abandoned railway station and the old port, and beyond them to the Tranquebar fort and a brushline of beach.

The plain white buildings of the dormitories and classrooms formed a quadrangle at the back. The girls kept it very neat, packing away their bedrolls each morning, sweeping the yard and watering the plants each evening. Only a few of them were actually orphans; most came from destitute families in the surrounding villages.

Helga pointed out a man who lay sleeping on the ground close to the gate. He was the father of one of the girls. He had TB and she helped him out. She was in control of a fund of charitable money which was donated by congregations in Germany and Sweden. Though the policy followed the contemporary line, that the money should be used to enable people to help themselves and not to encourage dependency, she found that hand-outs were sometimes unavoidable.

This man was a landless villager. He had a wife and other children. 'What can I do? The man is ill. If I do not give him money and help him now, then the whole family will become dependent on me. To go to the hospital in Mayuram costs ten rupees in bus fares, to get an X-ray, forty-five rupees. The best he can earn as a coolie is sixteen rupees a day. And that is only if he can find work.

'Of course, he cannot read and he cannot talk with the doctors. Twice he has discharged himself from hospital and I have had to look after him, giving him his medicine here at the orphanage. On Saturdays he comes here for food because he knows that we have meat on Saturdays. The food is more important than the medicine. Today he came for food, then lay down in the yard and did not go home. I think he is too weak.'

When her car took us home later, she arranged for the driver to drop him by his village. He was emaciated. The oblique view I had of his face in the seat before me was of bone jutting over cavernous cheek. When he got out to walk down the track, he looked back to me and made the Indian gesture of parting, hands joined beneath the chin. His eyes were red and dazed.

TB was rife in the villages. Helga spoke of another patient, a sixteen-year-old boy whose father had died. 'I asked his mother if he was getting his medicine. Some days, the mother said. I asked why. She said it was because he could not take the medicine on an empty stomach. If he did so it made him sick. So he took it only on the days when he had something to eat. That is, on the days after the days when she found work.'

There were other times when she could not help. She told me the story of a Christian girl who took up with a Hindu boy when her husband went to work in the tea gardens in Kerala. When the husband returned there was a row and a reconciliation. But he went back to Kerala, and after a time she went back to the Hindu boy, whom she must have loved, entering into a form of marriage that included the tying of the ritual thali around her neck. The next time the husband returned he refused to take her back and in a meeting of the panchayat she was thrown out of the village. Thus she was at once made homeless and excluded from society, family and Hindu lover. 'At last, she came to me. She wanted six hundred rupees. She had been told

155

that if she paid the panchayat members six hundred rupees so they could have a party and a drink or two, they would let her return to the village and reconcile her with her husband. But here I felt I could not help. What would people say if I gave good Lutheran deutschmarks to a faithless wife, to bribe a pack of drunkards?'

People came to Helga all day long. They knelt on the floor and wept before her and asked for work, help, money. They came to ask for wives for their sons from among her girls and workers. She had been responsible for arranging some marriages, supervising the acutely embarrassing interview when prospective bride and groom sneak looks across the room and attempt to size one another up.

'A co-worker I was fond of married recently. The girl came to me after the couple had their first row. She was despairing; she found it hard to be a wife, she knew that it was for the wife to obey. Then the man came to me in even greater distress; he could not understand that she should differ from him. Later, when six months pregnant, the woman had a black eye and told me that she had had an accident. But the husband came to me crying: what was wrong, why would his wife not obey him?'

Helga said that the Bible seemed close in India. Not just the goats or the way of life. It became easy to picture a messiah with a band of disciples, the gathering of multitudes; the miracles even seemed somehow less unlikely. She found that things she had previously read over or taken as metaphor gained direct meaning. We had been to a service in a remote village. Visiting the huts after it was over, she met a Christian woman who had not attended. Helga asked why. The woman became embarrassed, and her answer embarrassed all the other women around her. She had her period. Menstruating women were regarded as unclean and not permitted to enter temples or mosques. 'But we are Christians,' said Helga, and she told the story of Jesus curing the woman with the flow of blood. In India she found a special significance in the story: Jesus had let the woman touch him; to him she was not unclean.

They were new Christians in a new church. The service had been chaotic, the pastor forced to wait two hours as people milled around and half a dozen babies were collected up for a mass baptism. I wandered around, past brown mud huts webbed with the green gloss of pumpkin leaves. One of Helga's senior Bible-readers gave the congregation a dressing down. 'How long has this church been here? How long have you been Christians? How can you behave so badly?' Like a small grey thundercloud, she stormed them into silence.

All the congregation were adidravida. They seemed content to be treated like naughty children. They had no expectation of equality. The sermon was spoken slowly and full of images like a child's story. The church, a simple concrete hut with a corrugated iron roof, was painted inside with a jungle mural: an arkful of lions and tigers, elephants and monkeys painted by a fourteen-year-old boy. When the first service had been held there one of the women had exclaimed that it was almost as nice as a Hindu temple.

Helga stood godmother to one of the babies and his parents invited us to a celebration in their hut. Twenty women and children crowded in through the low door. They sat on the earth floor, spattered with the light that penetrated the weave of palm thatch. The father was the only man present, standing silently at the back. He was happy at last to have a son. His wife was a slight girl of twenty. This had been her fifth pregnancy in less than five years. She had had two stillbirths, two babies that died soon after birth. The pregnancies had come in too rapid succession, the husband deaf to medical advice, refusing contraception, returning to her before she had time to recover. The doctor himself had been surprised when the healthy boy was born. She made tea for us, heating it in an aluminium pan on the clay range. The flat top of the range was decorated with looped kolam designs in white chalk, and burning wood glowed in the round opening at floor level. The hut was very tidy, the range at one end, the granary in the centre, a tapering clay cylinder that was raised off the floor and reached almost to the roof but contained only a few inches of rice, and the sleeping area to the other end.

We were garlanded and brought chairs to sit on. One of the women relations passed round a dish piled high with granulated sugar, of which we ate pinches taken between our fingers. Then they brought bananas and boiled sweets. It was best not to calculate what that tiny hospitality cost them. Afterwards we prayed, led by the Bible-reader. The women knelt, drew the folds of their saris over their

157

bowed heads, and kept up a constant and unintelligible murmur throughout the prayer: stostostos. It was a corruption of the phrase 'stottiram', Praise the Lord, with which they had heard the Pentecostal Christians punctuate their prayers.

There were fifteen Lutheran households among the hundred or so in the settlement, and fifteen Pentecostal. The village proper was a quarter of a mile away, down a rough track through the fields. That was where people of caste lived. Our car had been left there, close to the road, and we had had to walk to the adidravida settlement where the church was. The conversion of adidravida was a threat to the village structure and often met hostility from the establishment. In another village nearby, the panchayat had that week prohibited Christians from drawing water from the communal well and also prohibited their employment. Already, two recent converts there had reverted to Hinduism.

A Hindu view was put to me by the clerk who dealt with my foreign exchange at the Indian Bank. She was a young woman in her twenties, bright, very pretty, college educated. While she checked the currency rates she gave Tom a rubber stamp and a used envelope so he could play at banking on the floor between her towers of ledgers. She spoke gently but her meaning was strong.

'A Hindu converted is an Indian taken away from the Mother, from India. A Muslim must join the world of Islam, a Christian is guided by the West.'

The ideology was that of Hindu radicalism, and of proud nonaligned India. And it was widespread, particularly in the north. A Delhi minister had recently let slip a remark that the Indian Christians might as well leave for Europe or America, and the ensuing controversy had not diminished his popularity.

Hinduism was a political identity as well as a religion, a philosophy, a social system and whatever else. It had shaped India's independence even while the constitution of independent India pronounced its secularity. It was inextricable from Indian life, threaded through from the mystic to the banal, amorphous, pluralistic, more flexible than any monotheism. Neither Christianity nor Periyar's cries could more than dent it. On Friday afternoons the staff did puja at the

Indian Bank, rang bells, made offerings and burnt camphor on a brass tray before the images grouped on the wall behind their desks: various configurations of Sarasvati, Lakshmi and Ganesh, plus the minarets of Mecca and Our Lady of Vailankanni. But the generosity extended to alien gods had its limits.

23

In mid-January came the Tamil holiday of Pongal. Sheikh Allauddin, free from his office in Karikal, sat cross-legged before his door and talked with those who passed down King Street. A group of men had gathered, leaning against the veranda wall. One stood astride his bicycle. Newspapers in their hands, they talked of America going to war against Iraq in the Persian Gulf.

Sheikh Allauddin called me over.

'So will there be war?' I asked.

'There is no one who says there will not be.'

'And what do you think about it?'

'I am Muslim. In Madras the Muslims have posted slogans on the walls, We love you Saddam. The Iraqi leader is now their hero.' He smiled diplomatically, raised a hand on which he wore a turquoise ring. 'I would not go so far, but Iraq has always been good to India. Now, if I am Muslim, you are British. Do you think this war is good?'

The man on the bike cut in. 'This war is good. America is too big. Britain also.' Everyone laughed. 'I am with Saddam.'

'But are you a Muslim?'

He had soft Tamil features beneath hair streaked with grey. He leant on to his handlebars and cackled at the thought.

Someone else answered for him. 'He's a Hindu.'

Shahabudeen shared their view. The general agreement seemed to be that Saddam Hussein was a man – his faults perhaps making him only more of a man – and Iraq was brave, while Saudi and Kuwait and the rest of the Gulf states were decadent in their wealth and cowardly to depend on America. The sense of Third World solidarity was almost as strong as Muslim fellow-feeling, and was heightened by simple machismo.

As the war progressed feeling for Saddam strengthened, the more as he seemed the more likely to lose. America's allies, Britain and

France, were the old colonial powers, and all three were referred to in the press as the 'Western imperialists', that phrase loaded with historical resentment. Each day, pages of photographs in the Tamil papers showed flesh-and-blood Iraqis on one side, women and children as well as soldiers, and on the other, the steel of sophisticated American weaponry. In a village where cars were rare and even the electricity supply sporadic, the contrast had an emotional charge. At the end of January, Tranquebar had its own anti-American demonstration, a ripple of those in Madras and the northern cities. A band of boys, mainly Muslims, hung around on the bridge by the bus stand carrying scrawled placards, and later trickled down King Street to the football pitch before the fort.

Being Christians, Wilson and his sons had some sympathy with the West. Morning and evening they listened to the BBC news. I listened with them, going into the passageway outside their open window when I heard the tones of the World Service signature.

The day the war broke out, I had gone to Karikal to buy a radio for myself; but there were none to be found, even in the foreign market. When I returned, only two hours after the formal declaration, I found that the price of the auto-rickshaw back to Tranquebar had risen by ten rupees. In the past, bargaining had often started at fifty rupees and dropped from there, but this time it stuck. Petrol had gone up to twelve rupees a litre.

I asked why.

'Saddam!' came the answer. Merchants had jumped ahead of the news and increased prices, and already petrol was near unavailable. Transport in India was always hectic but after a while you took that for granted; then a tremor hinted how close real disorder lay, as if what you always suspected were true, that the whole infrastructure might suddenly disintegrate.

The auto-rickshaw boys were excited about the war. Words like 'bombing' and 'missile' ricocheted through their English vocabulary. Karikal auto drivers wore bellbottom trousers and long-tailed shirts that were cut tight across their chests. They talked with as much bravado as they drove. To top up his tank for the journey, one driver siphoned some petrol from a friend's engine into an empty half-bottle

161

of whisky he kept stashed by his seat. The container was part of the image: taxi-drivers, who were hardened men beside the auto boys, kept water for their engines in full-size whisky bottles tucked into the passenger doors. All through the outskirts of Karikal, the driver stopped at roadside shops to look for more fuel. When the auto finally stalled, just before it reached the house, he only laughed: he would walk to Porayar to continue the hunt.

That same evening my former servant Shivaharmi came down the street carrying an empty kerosene can.

'*Ilae, ilae.*' Her free hand rolled over to underline her negative.

There was no kerosene to be had at the subsidised shop by the Schwartz hostel, or anywhere else in Tranquebar, and for her, if not for the driver, it was far from a game. By the first of February, the price of kerosene and of other basic commodities had risen by thirty-three per cent. The fragile economy of the village – though it was superficially so insular – had nothing to cushion it from distant events.

Just then, a local political crisis hit Tamil Nadu.

Each week the Indian national papers carried the story of a political upheaval somewhere across the country, whether the fall of a state government or some procedural row or assembly walk-out that put a ruling coalition under threat. Each state had its own political parties, the abbreviations for which jammed the editorials: strings of initials that grew ever longer as the original parties splintered and re-formed. To an outsider, their names and characteristics were as hard to remember and identify as those of the minor dynasties of pre-Mughal India – though the dynasties had had a longer time-span. No one stopped to explain who stood for what. Party loyalty generally ran along lines of race, religion and caste, while social and economic issues too often lay submerged beneath the soap opera of the struggle of individuals for power, the alliances, plots and manoeuvres. Ideology seemed an accessory to the personae of the leading politicians, personae which were sometimes reduced to cartoon level for the easy consumption of the illiterate.

In Tamil Nadu there was M. Karunanidhi, the DMK leader, called MK, a bloated figure in moustache and dark glasses. His features were commoner on Tamil postcards than those of contemporary film stars – but he had been in films himself before he turned to politics. His chief opponent was Ms. Jayalalitha of the AIADMK. She had been an actress. While villagers revered her as 'the primordial power', some critics had dubbed her Queen Victoria. She was a stout woman with a podgy face and hair drawn back tight from a centre parting. Though the DMK had regained power with a majority in the state election of 1988, in the Indian general election of the following year an alliance of the main opposition parties, the AIADMK and Congress, had taken every Tamil Nadu seat.

Two years on, the opposition alliance was more impatient than ever to bring about a new state election. As normal measures had so far failed, they resorted to Gandhian tactics and announced a plan for a general agitation, or rasta roko, in protest against the DMK government, to take place on the twenty-eighth of January. Their action was pre-empted by the state government, which withdrew public transport from the roads from the previous evening until the following morning, had trains cancelled, and took into preventive custody twenty-five thousand people, including many politicians. The measures were ostensibly to prevent stone-throwing and arson. In Tranquebar every shop and stall kept its boards up, chained and padlocked, and not a car was to be seen on the main road.

At midnight on the thirtieth, the central government in Delhi dismissed the state government and imposed direct rule. The move was said to have been directed from behind the scenes by Rajiv Gandhi, who was Jayalalitha's Congress ally. It was universally perceived as purely political, its pretext, the supposed breakdown of law and order in the state, too thin for examination. There was uproar in the media, and in the villages there was silence. For the second time in a week, people were taken into detention and public transport was ordered off the roads.

That day I walked the couple of kilometres to Thaiub Ali's garden at Kathan Savadi. No autos or private cars were running, and the hired bicycles at the shops by the bus stand had all been taken before eight in the morning. There were only cyclists and walkers on the road, strung across the tarmac ahead where it cut a straight line through the rice fields. They drifted down its centre. There was no need to listen for the horn and the unbraking motor that on normal days would drive them scuttling for the verge.

Thaiub Ali was happy to see the back of the DMK, however unconstitutionally it had come about. The day before, when he was praying, the idea had come to him that he must put the Congress party symbol on the wall by his door. He had drawn it in sandal paste, the yellow outline of a raised hand, with lifeline and creases at the finger joints, alongside Rajiv's photo.

The following week, the left-wing parties in Tamil Nadu called a general strike in protest at the central government takeover. The day before, another twenty-three or twenty-five thousand were rounded up, this time members of the DMK and leftists. We had another day of silence: public services were closed down, shops were shut and hardly anyone got to work. You could not say though who closed in protest and who out of caution. Fear was widespread, though no more than a handful of incidents had been reported outside the cities, a couple of buses burned and a stone-throwing here or there.

One afternoon a few days later the shops were locked again at the bus stand. It was hot and clusters of men stood round in the dust along the road. They did not look like men waiting for buses. They stood too still, too intent, for that. I recognised some students from the teacher training college and asked what was going on. They called it a strike. All the shopkeepers in the village had closed in protest over something, but at what they didn't say.

One of the students caught up with me as I walked back. Alone, he told me more. A few hours earlier a youth had been seen stealing from one of the shops. The merchants went after him and a battle had developed between the merchants and the boys who hung around the bus stand. They threw stones and wielded broken soda bottles but I could not discover whether anyone was much hurt. The police had come and broken up the fight and taken people away. The bystanders waited now for another row to start when the police and the merchants returned. The student said the brawl was not unusual: something like this happened every two or three months. This was modern India. A violent undercurrent ran just beneath the surface always.

*　　*　　*

Thaiub Ali had told me that one of my neighbours was arrested before the first demonstration against the DMK.

'Which neighbour?'

'Oudoumane. From the big house next to you on Queen Street.'

That was Sheikh Allauddin's uncle.

'He went with the police on Sunday night, and I think that he has now been released. He is the Congress Party President for Tranquebar.'

That explained his presence at local functions, at TELC weddings and funerals. Thaiub Ali was senior to him in the party, at Tanjore district level.

'His position has no real power attached, I must tell you. It is only temporary.'

I said that I had heard gossip about him.

'To be honest with you, he is the very worst fellow.' Thaiub Ali's daughters giggled at that. 'He has a reputation. And as Congress Party President he may accept the donations for buildings, community projects and suchlike. This is unfortunate. Congress is very shamed.'

'Is it true he has two wives?'

'There is one who is Muslim. One is not Muslim. Harijan, backward caste. Yet he is a relative of our family.' So the shame, or at least the embarrassment, may also have been personal.

Although I had seen Oudoumane many times – on his veranda, on the step before his door, riding down the street sidesaddle on the back of a bicycle pedalled by a boy – it had come to seem unlikely that I would meet him. I decided to contrive an introduction, and helped Tom throw a ball over his garden wall.

At home he wore colours, a blue and green striped lungi instead of the formal white dhoti. He had not shaved, white bristles showing among the black around his thin moustache, and his hair was unoiled. He had a narrow, mobile face, pockmarked skin and yellowish eyes. A quick laugh suggested cleverness.

His arrest had been well-mannered. He had been out when the Porayar police called, the day that the DMK were rounding people up before the rasta roko agitation. They left a message. Next morning he went to see them, to be taken on a bus to Trichy.

'I have been to gaol three times. Always for political reasons, that I make clear. There is a title – Thiyagi. It is given to a man who was gaoled for his part in the independence struggle, in the British period. I carry that title.'

I realised that he looked different at home because he was not wearing his Nehru cap.

In 1943, when he was a student at Porayar college, he was arrested by the British authorities and spent a month in prison at Kumbakonam. In 1976 (the year of the Emergency) he had first become Congress Party President at Tranquebar, and in 1978, at the same time as Indira Gandhi was herself arrested under Janata rule, he was gaoled for six days at Trichy. Now he had spent another four days in the Trichy gaol, along with ninety others from Porayar and Tranquebar.

'Have the prisons changed?'

'Very much. Under the British, conditions were hard. There were eight to ten of us crammed into a small cell. Now it is much better. There is a large area. You can move around. It is freer. Even the food is better. And that is under the DMK!'

Oudoumane's house had been built by his family in 1937. They had demolished the Danish house on the site, which they had purchased from Hindus. The new building's French colonial style was probably influenced by the architecture of Saigon, where he said his father had dealt in diamonds.

We sat on the veranda on a wooden bench. Creeper had over-run the garden, swathing shapes that might equally have been shrubs or debris and stuck up now like knees under a blanket. The creeper had sprays of tiny pink flowers. Tendrils reached to the wheels of a blue-painted cart that stood on the track that ran to the outside gate. There was an Enfield motorcycle on the ver-anda, and a bicycle by the door into the house, propped on to its stand. The door was plain wood but someone had painted a design around the opening, a broad band of blue broken by wave shapes in green and yellow and pink. The walls were a faded greenish turquoise.

The woman I assumed was his Muslim wife brought coffee.

166

She was grey haired and slow moving, with a long, rather haggard face.

'I was myself in Vietnam, staying there twenty years by intervals. Twenty years in all. In 1973 I returned here to Tranquebar. My family lost much in Vietnam. We had property and wetlands. Our circumstances were reduced.

'There was land here also. I still have some wetlands just outside the village. This year we had some rice off them but not much. I had two brothers and it has been difficult for me to manage the land in a satisfactory way. They were interfering. Once, I tell you, I had to fast in order to resolve a dispute in the family. My brothers had ideas about the cultivation with which I could not agree. For ten days I took nothing but water, and at the end of ten days they came to me and settled.'

The old Gandhian laughed. 'But my two brothers are now expired.'

He showed me the ruinous house. Fissures ran across the high ceilings of the formal rooms that faced on to Queen Street. The floor above he said was unsafe. 'Beams we sell in eight-foot lengths, for two hundred and fifty rupees. Bricks we sell separately.' All that remained standing was the concrete shell of the 1930s structure, and lumps of that were breaking away from the rusting steel joists.

It was many years since the family had occupied the whole house. The front section had at one time held the offices of the Indian Bank, and at another, the co-operative store. At the back were three or four small dark rooms leading off a courtyard. Oudoumane said that was all they needed, with his two sons and his two daughters.

We returned to the veranda and he pointed out the rust stain spreading across the crumbling ceiling. That too would come down.

And the garden?

'This we do not need. This land we shall sell.'

Regina Mary said that only the first wife, the Muslim, was living at the house, though the children were by the second wife. 'The Muslim one cannot have children but I think that he has affection for her.' The Hindu wife lived in one of the houses up by the mosque.

167

Regina Mary's brothers thought that there were other women too.

Wilson overheard us talking. He put his head round the gate. 'That man is not liked. Nobody speaks with him. It is on account of his morality.'

24

Point Calimere, down the coast, was famous as a site for wintering birds. I planned to go there, and take Shahabudeen and the girls, but the trip was delayed and then postponed again because of the strikes. When we did get there most of the birds had flown north.

'Too late again, Shaha. Our timing is not good.'

'There is next year. The birds will return.'

'I may not.'

'Then there is the year after. We will be sure to come before the end of January.'

We filed along a narrow dyke. The guide from the nature reserve listed the thousands of birds we might have seen a week before, many kinds of duck, storks and flamingoes. Shaha followed at his shoulder; he held his hands behind his back and kept his head raised as if to look a long way off. The mudflats were bare. Fingers of water reached into them and spread in the distance. Only the sandpipers remained, stepping neatly in the mud and puncturing it with their straight beaks. Behind us came Jebin and Marhin in Singapore frocks of stunning yellow. They wore no shoes but white socks which were plastered with mud. Jebin wore the guide's binoculars around her neck, raised them at times to look through first one end and then the other, to try the effect. Her mother and older sisters stepped carefully, lifting their skirts above the ground.

We had left before five, to arrive soon after dawn. Point Calimere is the southern tip of the Coromandel coast, eighty or a hundred kilometres south of Tranquebar. By the time it grew light we were in monotonous wetland, straw-coloured rice fields stretching in all directions. But that soon gave way. On the east, between us and the sea, a range of odd sandy hills erupted. For a while the road ran between these and a geometric landscape of salt beds. The hills at last smoothed into the open grassland of the nature reserve. There was a lighthouse and, just round the point, a fishing harbour on a rivermouth, a beach where clouds of black flies hovered over fish that were split flat and laid to dry. The Jaffna Peninsula and Sri Lanka lay fifty kilometres to the south across the Palk Strait. To the west, the coast along the Strait was marsh and mudflat, broken by innumerable small branches of the Cauvery.

Going back at noon, we stopped and walked up one of the hills. At its summit was a Hindu pavilion covering what were supposed to be footprints of Rama – unlikely relics since they were raised rather than indented, and no larger than Marhin's feet, which were bare now since she had rid herself of her socks in the run up the hill. When I made the comparison, Marhin climbed into the pavilion as if to try the prints for their exact size. Shirin pulled her back. Her look was severe. A god's feet were not to be measured, whatever his religion.

The hill gave a view across the salt beds, a level grid that ran to the horizon. White cones of salt were set at intervals along the lines between the squares, and at wider intervals, huge pyramids. There was no shade. Coolies worked the beds in gangs, shoulder to shoulder, treading the mud and tamping the surface smooth with wooden tools. There were men and women but mainly women; it was slow labour and women came cheaper. The men wore little but rags wound around their heads and loins; the women, cotton saris whose colours defied the mud.

As we approached Nagapattinam I remembered something Shaha had said that morning when I was half asleep. Something about people who were afflicted by devils and a mosque where the devils were cast out. He had described how the possessed were held in chains and my mind had conjured up an historical bedlam. I had thought it a thing of the past. But when we returned by the place where he had spoken of the mosque, I realised: in India such a story need not be history.

We turned off the road down a straight dirt track, a kilometre to the village. It was called Papavoordurga, the mosque more correctly a durga, the burial place of the Sheikh Allauddin Uliulla.

Shaha asked what I knew about affliction by devils.

I said I thought of it as a kind of insanity.

'No. In your country do you not have people who are afflicted by devils?'

'We think of them as crazy.'

Bhanu said, 'These are not crazy. Like crazy, but crazy is different. Devils are when a boy or girl, man or woman dies, and they take the body of an ordinary person.'

'It is more than that,' said Shaha. 'Devils are like saints. But saints do good things. Devils are dangerous.'

The durga lay at the end of a narrow square lined with poor Muslim houses. It was a simple building, a large open hall raised up steps, with a railed enclosure at one end before the saint's tomb. Faded paper pennants hung from the rafters between wooden columns. Half a dozen fat Muslims in crocheted skullcaps skulked beside offering boxes at the entrance and at the steps to the tomb itself. Most of the people sheltering in the hall appeared to be Hindu. They were obviously poor villagers, thin, small, dark, their faces drawn. They dozed on straw mats, perhaps fifty women and children and a few men. They did not look possessed, only tired.

'It is the men who are most dangerous, because of their strength.' Shaha pointed to a pavilion nearby, another open pillared hall. Twenty or thirty men sat there in the shade of the wide roof. So long as they were still it was not obvious that they wore leg irons, each man shackled to one of the whitewashed pillars. Then one of them caught sight of my white face and the child I held on my hip. He stood up with a clank of chains, and a shudder passed through the group. One after another, they cried out and waved their hands. They were suddenly so disturbing that I turned Tom's head and carried him away.

'How do they come here?' I asked Shaha.

'Their families bring them. They know about this place. People come from villages a long way off, even from other districts. If one of their family is afflicted, they bring him. The man is chained here for one week, one month, three months, years, until he is cured.'

'And are they cured?'

'One day comes. They go home.'

'How does this happen?'

171

'I cannot tell. Only that one day they are afflicted with the devil and the next day he is gone. It is by the power of the saint.'

He seemed to think I was disappointed. 'But you must come one Wednesday evening. You must see how they act then. You cannot imagine if you do not see yourself how strong they are.' He clenched his fists and mimed a man breaking his bonds. 'They twist, turn, roll on the ground, drag their chains. Four men could not hold them.'

'On Wednesdays?'

'Wednesday evenings after seven.'

'Why then?'

'I cannot say. Only that this happens. I have seen it many times.'

At Nagore, Shaha insisted we stop at the mosque. He said there was something I must see. Close to the entrance was a railed area I had not noticed before. Displayed on its walls were framed groups of objects like surrealist collages, each collection including a written paper: pieces of bone as long as fingers, arrays of pins, needles and nails, scraps of metal, stones, razor blades, hens' eggs.

'When a person is afflicted with a devil he sometimes vomits. And when the devil is chased out he vomits up many strange things. In this mosque also there was a saint who had power over devils. Here is the evidence. Each piece is accompanied by the testimony of the man who was cured.'

I asked how people came to swallow these things in states of possession. But Shaha had never considered that.

'Why do you always ask questions? Do you not see the saint's power?'

An evening soon after, we were on the beach. It grew dark as we talked, sitting on the bleached timbers of a catamaran. The children were playing by the waves. Jebin and Marhin caught the little crabs and brought them to Tom, crabs with grey shells that were so insubstantial as to be almost transparent, and coral eyes on stalks. They whisked off before he could hold them.

'India is different,' said Shaha. The phrase was trite. It was a slogan the Indian Tourist Board once used. I remembered the grey of a winter afternoon in London and a poster on the underground: a doorway that must have been in Rajasthan, a man in a saffron turban caught in a shaft of light, and the slogan beneath. But Shaha meant it. 'India is the only country where there are signs. Each and everywhere you find them, like at that durga, like at Nagore. Or like that saint I told you of before.'

Once he believed he had seen this saint's aura. He was praying in a room with him. The saint, sitting absolutely still, had first looked directly at him, then turned his eyes down and away. After some minutes, Shaha did not know how many, he found that when he looked towards the saint, he could no longer see his features. His eyes were misted and he could see only that the man's form was bathed in a violet glow.

'I was introduced to that man by a good friend. His name was Khalil Muhammad and he came from Vellore near Madras. He could see things before they happened. How is this possible? An example. He was in Singapore. He was to fly from Singapore to Madras. Five minutes before the plane was to leave he was at my cousin's house. My cousin says, Are you crazy? Why do you not catch your plane? It takes twenty, twenty-five minutes to get to the airport. No need, my friend says, the plane will fly later. My cousin challenges him and they go to the airport. The plane had left on time but there was some technical problem; it returned ten minutes later. After one hour the fault was corrected and the plane took off again, with my friend on board.

'Again, we were on the beach at Nagapattinam. I had something in my hand and threw it into the sea. He says, You throw that in the sea, a cyclone will come. He had a way of pulling at his beard. He'd pull at a hair, like this, and he'd say, So, Shahabudeen, so it is. The next morning I heard the radio. I heard that a cyclone was forming, that there was a ridge of low pressure, et cetera. Now, how is this possible?'

He pointed at Marhin. 'And she has it too. One day, one or two years ago, we saw great clouds in the sky. It will be raining somewhere, I said. Yes, she answered, it rains in Pondicherry. That was at five o'clock. At seven, seven-fifteen, the radio says that it rained five inches in Pondicherry. That is one example. There are many others. How? She was only a baby, not four years old.'

173

25

Around that time the *Indian Express* carried the story of the murder of a sorcerer in a neighbouring district. It was widely known that the dead man had been practising witchcraft. When his family suffered a series of misfortunes, people had said that he had upset the evil spirits by his activity and that they were taking their revenge. Two of his sons died. The third son, Muthukumar, quarrelled with him, saying that none of the family would prosper until he gave up his sorcery. Muthukumar left home and went to the town and set up a little shop by the bus stand. Muthukumar's business failed, and then the marriage he had arranged for himself was called off. One night soon after, someone poured kerosene over the sorcerer as he slept and set him ablaze. Muthukumar was arrested.

The story got a fraction of a column on an inside page, reported in a matter-of-fact provincial style. There was no hint of wonder at the motive ascribed to the accused, which was apparently as self-explanatory, as ordinary, as the motive of sexual jealousy behind a domestic murder in Europe.

Almost four hundred years earlier, the Icelander Jon Olafsson, sentry at the fort on the beach, knew of as many sorcerers at Copenhagen as at Tranquebar.

For the first Europeans in India, the physical surroundings contained much that was entirely new. When Olafsson wanted to describe something to his Icelandic readers, he could take his comparisons only from the limited frame of reference that was their direct experience: a banana for example had to be a buttery fruit, about the size of a guillemot hung to dry. The spirit world of Tranquebar, however, was not a novelty. Signs, spells and devils had as real an existence for Icelander as they had for Indian.

With Olafsson at Tranquebar was a Dutch carpenter called Cornelius. He was regarded as a good man, a fine craftsman and an excellent singer. But then a Spanish dollar went missing in the mess and an Indian sorcerer revealed him as the culprit, and one night he was seen to have intercourse with a goat. He fled the colony. Olafsson remembered him with pity, recalling how insomnia would drive him from his bunk and how he would return weeping, apparently tortured by his nocturnal wanderings. He did not hold Cornelius responsible. His crimes, he explained, were the result of a spell cast by an evil sorceress in Holland whose granddaughter he had jilted.

Then there was Hans, the ship's cook on the homeward voyage, who ran amok on board and eventually killed the rector just before they landed at Ireland. When faced with the penalty, Hans threw into the sea a mysterious piece of paper and said that he was prepared for death: he announced the end of a twenty-one-year pact with the devil.

In those days, Tranquebar had a resident native exorcist. Olafsson had watched him work, calling up a possessing spirit by striking a resounding piece of copper close to the ear of the victim, then negotiating the conditions for its departure, haggling over the quantity and frequency of sacrifices and offerings of capons, rice and betel.

The German pastoress Eva Maria had witnessed cases of apparent possession in India.

'I can offer no words of explanation. Only that there is more in the world than we accept in the West. Scepticism must stop somewhere.'

And exorcism?

Her husband Johnson had heard of the durga by Nagapattinam. A Tamil paper had recently published a letter from an educated Muslim, demanding that funds be provided to enable the establishment to extend its successful healing work among the 'mentally deranged'.

Wilson was said to have power to cast out devils. The whole village knew the story of the wife of the bank clerk, who was possessed, and who was cured when Wilson prayed over her. One of Wilson's former pupils told me of a case that had occurred some years before, when he was still headmaster at the school.

'A boy was affected by a demon, the spirit of a woman who had lived in his house and had died three months before. This boy had a fit, tried to throw himself into the well. Though he was just a boy, no one could hold him. He cried out, again and again, that "she" was calling him to the well. At last four men had him pinioned down. Wilson came and held the Bible out to him but the boy threw it back in his face, screaming, "I hate him. I will kill him." Wilson was very calm. He prayed for a long time until the boy was quiet. The boy had such seizures repeatedly over the course of six months but finally, as a result of continuous prayer, he was freed of the demon.'

Was this just psychological power, sheer force of character, or was it something more? Eva Maria spoke of a time when she had gone to a service in a remote village and a child came running up to her saying there was a devil in the church. She found a woman there having a fit, rolling over and over, quite out of her mind. They brought the woman back to Tranquebar. Wilson was called in, prayed and laid the Bible on the woman's head. For two hours the fit continued, or the devil fought.

'The atmosphere grew more and more tense, with the woman screaming and Wilson booming away at the Bible, and at last I could not stand it. I became exasperated and I got up and I shouted in German, Get out of here you devil, whoever you are! And suddenly the woman was still. It was very strange, particularly since I knew that no one in the room could understand German. I do not like to think too much about it.'

Wilson was surprised when I showed doubt about devils. 'You do not believe in devils? Do you not read the Bible? In the Bible there are many people whose devils are cast out.'

He had become known among Hindus and Christians as both an exorcist and a healer. Each day he made some journey out from the retirement of his veranda. He would fold aside his newspaper and go indoors to change his lungi for pressed grey trousers and put on a shirt over his vest, brush back his silver hair and take out his long-range specs. Then he would wheel his bicycle down the passage before our gate. He was going to Thirukaddiyur to give a tutorial, or somewhere else in the service of what he called individual evangelism.

'I work chiefly with the non-Christians.'

'How? Do people come to you?'

'When I am on my travels, on the road or in a bus, people come and they ask my help and by the goodness of God I can cure them. In the name of the Lord. I say a prayer over them and anoint them with oil. And the Lord works through me. He tells me: Wilson, touch this man, heal this disease, and I carry out these actions. Jesus is there with me. It is a marvellous thing.' His smile was as measured and public as his speech. The pause wanted alleluias to fill it. 'And by my presence I will sow a seed. And in time they will follow the way I lead.'

It was said that some years before Wilson himself had gone through a healing experience. He had some kind of stroke or paralysis on one side of the face which had been cured as suddenly as it had come. Since that time his Christianity – and perhaps his personality too – had altered. The man who had been appointed headmaster of the boys' school had been altogether more conventional, a disciplinarian, even an occasionally intimidating figure, but a plain upstanding member of the TELC congregation. His brand of non-denominational evangelism had been developed only since the illness. He gave up attending church, read the Bible, and acquired his visionary fire.

Once he offered me the benefits of his direct line. 'Each morning as you know from five to six I am praying on the roof above, under the sky. If there is something you need, ask me and I will pray for you.'

177

26

In astrology, Saturn is an adverse planet. As the Hindu god Sani, his influence is almost universally malign. When his eye touched on the baby Ganesh, the child of Shiva and Parvati, the baby's head was severed from its body, to be replaced with the elephant's head by which Ganesh or Ganpaty became known. The vengeful Parvati cursed Sani and withered his leg in return, so that the god must limp in his slow passage around the zodiac, taking two and a half years to pass from sign to sign.

Sani's temple at Thirunallar near Karikal celebrates each transit into a new sign with a festival that draws tens of thousands of devotees. Most of them come directed by their astrologers, to placate Sani as he enters their ruling house. A man on the bus we took from Karikal had a problem at work. He was a railwayman from Madras; he had done his job well for five years and was in line for promotion but quite unexpectedly someone had been brought in from another district and appointed over his head. His astrologer had suggested that a trip to Thirunallar would sort it out. A night on the train each way and a few hours' bus ride, a morning queueing to gain a glimpse of the idol, a bathe in the tank: the weekend would be worth it if his prospects looked up.

People jammed the road, villagers and city people in Western clothes. An Ambassador car tried to force a way through, made no ground, disgorged two businessmen, plump and balding with triple white stripes elegantly applied to their foreheads. Side by side they made an even passage through the crowd. There was command in their presence. Shaha and I walked in their wake.

The streets were banked with stalls selling standard festival goods: plastic toys, cheap idols, cooking utensils. A feature at Thirunallar were the astrological stalls, tables spread with almanacs (the official one for the surrounding districts was the No. 28 Cobra Mark), pamphlet predictions, pamphlets on Saturn. Young men at the road's edge offered a new fad: 'computer' predictions delivered by two-foot robots that packed up into old Samsonite suitcases, tin robots with square electric clocks for faces, dials on their chests. Their message was conveyed through rubbery headphones. 'Only a tape,' said Shaha disparagingly, 'but it costs only one rupee.' One rupee was a fair-ground sixpence, the price of a balloon, a toy windmill or a baby's rattle.

For an instant the crowd divided to pass a figure rattling a steel begging bowl. He stood fixed before it, like a rock in a torrent, a figure smeared in ash from head to foot, face androgynous and blank as that of a mime between acts. Across his bare chest, down his arms and down his legs dangled limes like yellow pompoms on a Pierrot. The limes were attached by pins stuck directly into the skin, which was pulled taut at each puncture point by the weight of the fruit. The passing crowd did not slow, but nor did it touch him. Against the stream came another carnival grotesque, wild haired, pop eyed, waggling a pink tongue from his mouth. The tongue was bloodlessly transfixed by a thick steel needle six inches long.

Mostly the crowd was composed and deliberate. They purchased tickets for darshan, the showing of the sacred idol held in the temple; like theatre tickets these ranged in price from five to ten and twenty rupees according to viewing distance. They bought coconuts and bananas as offerings for the deity, then attached themselves to the queue before whichever temple gate was designated by their ticket. These queues were so long that they doubled back on themselves, but they were patient lines which did not seem to require the smart Pondy Territory gendarmes to keep them in order, so ordinary that you would not have guessed their religious purpose. Overhead ranged the signs of shops and banks, eating-places and cheap lodg-ings. On the first floor above a tea stall, the Bright Future Tuition Centre, H.Sci., B.Com., would help to counteract Saturn's influence on examinations. On the ornate concrete balcony next door a board advertised the Sani Tourist Home. Thirunallar was a plain town and the temple was its chief business. It looked a prosperous small town, even for the Karikal district.

Shaha slipped between people, tall, thin, his white clothes uncreased and spotless. He touched nothing and it seemed that no one brushed against him. At the end of a long street we came to the sacred tank. He stopped to buy a single Gold Flake cigarette. The tank was huge and square, shallow steps running into the water along all sides. Ziegenbalg had recorded that in his day a man stood on his head in the centre of this tank for three hours each morning. Now hundreds of people thronged the steps. There was fervour in their washing. They scrubbed, oiled their bodies, shampooed their hair with sachets of Sunsilk that were sold alongside the traditional oil at the surrounding stalls. Some dipped underwater, gargled and prayed, immersed to their chests and raising hands to the back of their heads. At last they dressed again in new clothes and discarded the old ones. The centre of the tank was littered with cotton bundles and a boat circled there, a man fishing them out with a wooden pole. Thousands had bathed in the stagnant green water since the festival began a day before. Shaha sniffed. 'They do not mind.' A middle-class family went down the steps beside us as to a riverbank picnic, the boys undoing shirt buttons as they walked, the women laughing and loosening their hair. 'They believe the holy water will wash away their troubles.'

I sat on the steps and read ten ways to avert Saturn's evil eye. Change your name to the number five. Carve a yantra and make a kolam. Perform various recitations and pujas with blue flowers, sesame and other oils. Anoint the idol of Siva with milk taken from a black cow or from a cow which has a black tongue. On your birthday, present Vedic scholars with a black cow or at least a coconut. Wrap some sesame in a black silk cloth, sleep with it under the pillow, bathe in oil, add the sesame to freshly cooked rice and feed it to a crow.

Again at Thirunallar, I met a brahmin family from the town of Coimbatore. They came for the sake of their daughter, whose horoscope signalled the influence of Saturn over her for the next seven and a half years. The daughter was an intelligent girl of twenty. I sat beside her on the floor as the priests prepared to bring out the ancient Shiva lingam for which the temple was famous. It was a long wait, extended by a power cut. Forty pilgrims lined the walls of a narrow chamber at the heart of the temple. Without light or fan it had an underground

180

stuffiness. Brahmin priests slipped past, young men and old, bringing brass vessels, arranging the brass tray on which the lingam was to be placed. Their skin glowed amber from the lamps they carried.

The girl talked of how she had a better chance of making a career for herself in America than in Tamil Nadu. She was studying medicine. She was a conventional brahmin and had some brahmin religious knowledge but did not consider herself especially devout. Beyond morning puja, she did not think of religion much in the day. This pilgrimage to Thirunallar was important, however. The temple was not beautiful, like Chidambaram or Tanjore. Its carvings were not exceptional, its walls were caked with paint, its courtyards roofed with corrugated iron and railed like a cattle market. But Saturn's influence could not be overestimated. By her propitiation she intended to reduce the trouble the planet could cause in the next phase of her life, and specifically, cancel a threat that she might slide into irreligiousness.

She talked on in the close darkness. She speculated, 'If we did not believe in Saturn, he would not trouble us so.' She was scientifically trained. She did not share the literal, magical faith of the peasants. She allowed that a god's power could be subjective.

So could I say in return that his power did not exist – that the railwayman would not clear his way to promotion by coming to Thirunallar nor she escape trouble? A woman who was believed to be possessed by a devil, and herself believed it so, might indeed be cured by the touch of a Bible or the posthumous power of a Muslim holy man. And since a devil could be cast out once and for all, she might have a better chance of complete cure than a mental patient undergoing long therapy in England.

In the country about Tranquebar, gods and devils were alive for just about everyone, save the Town Rationalist Forum. Their power became almost palpable, as if amplified into objectivity by the collective consciousness. Shaha said that things happened in India that could not happen in other places. Wilson apparently cured the deranged. A Hindu stuck a needle through his tongue and did not bleed. There were some things that could be reasoned away or put down to plain chance or coincidence. There were others that could not. And Muslim, Christian and Hindu viewed them alike, with a shared perception that went beyond their individual beliefs. Between that enviably sure perception and the modern Western outlook – whether agnostic void or theistic doubt – lay a gulf greater than that between the religions themselves.

27

When Maya Sekar was studying for her matric, her mother made her do three hours' puja daily in the belief that this would win her total marks. Maya's schoolteachers stressed the efficacy of revision. Somehow she found time for both and she passed well enough. She thought now that too much time was wasted in religion.

But then Maya stood out among the villagers. She had been born at Tranquebar, a Nadar, but she had become educated and urban. For the last ten years she had lived in the north of India, in the industrial zone around Jamshedpur, not far from Calcutta. She said, in the south you see temples, in the north (her part of the north, anyway) you see factories.

She was staying at her mother's, in the three or four rooms that remained of the eighteenth-century house her grandfather had purchased. At the entrance, beyond the redundant bases of lost Danish columns, the doorframe bore a religious signature. Just above the step on each side was a painted band: the three horizontal white stripes of Shiva in a rectangle of yellow; the red dot of his consort Parvati in the centre; red dots again in the two white rectangles above and below. On the back door the stripes and dots were arranged in a circle for good luck.

A lean-to room at one end of the house was kept for puja. It was carefully arranged and very clean. A shelf set eighteen inches from the floor made a simple altar, with photographs and images propped behind a protective sheet of glass: a pantheon of gods, a guru, black and white studio portraits of Maya's late father and of Rao Bahadur Ratnasamy Nadar wearing turban, long coat and baggy white pants, seated and leaning on his cane.

There was another place for prayer in the garden. This was largely a thorn thicket, bordered by crumbling walls and adjoining an abandoned colonial cemetery. I sometimes came in that way, through a gap in the wall, and found Maya collecting firewood or washing clothes at the well. There were coconut palms and a papaya tree in the garden, an old jackfruit that had fallen almost on its side in the rains two years before, and the nim tree before which the shrine stood. A straight path cut there through the undergrowth and the ground within the enclosure was always freshly swept. The shrine was a low block built of bricks and clay, whitewashed and decorated with a stencilled pattern of elephants that also appeared on the walls of the house. Two further elephants were painted either side of its opening.

Maya's mother had cropped hair, peppered grey. It had been shorn in offering, and it emphasised her frailness and her austerity. She was old now but there had been a time when she would spend eight hours a day at puja. If she had two hundred rupees, she would spend a hundred and fifty on offerings, on incense, bananas, coconuts and oils. She would visit temples, do darshan. Every one or two years she made the journey to the Meenakshi temple at Madurai which was her favourite. She also went to the Protestant church. Years before, the Lutheran pastor, whose garden backed on to her street, gave her a Bible. Some mornings she read verses from the Gospels as puja. Her husband never begrudged the religious offerings but she had to hide the Bible from him as he did not approve of Christianity.

Maya possessed the same small frame as her mother, the long oval face and deep-set eyes. She had a baby due at the beginning of March and her pretty saris were wound discreetly across her hugeness. She too was frail; as her belly grew the rest of her seemed to become only more slender. She was stranded at Tranquebar because of ill-health. She had made the trip south at the end of December, with the two children she already had, to see her family and take her mother back with her to Jamshedpur so that she could help with the baby when it came. But she had not had the strength for the return journey, five more days on a stifling train. Sister Cicely at the nuns' hospital was treating her for anaemia and advised her to stay and have the baby there.

Her children didn't think much of the village. There was Meenakshi, namesake of her grandmother's goddess, a girl of eight, and Natraj who was five. In January Natraj fell off a bicycle and had to have twelve stitches in his knee. Maya said she could not rest for watching him. He fretted all day long. It was no wonder he had accidents.

'Constantly he is asking, when will we go back to Jamshedpur? Why is his daddy not coming home at four o'clock? Will his daddy come to say goodnight? He will speak only to me. He will stand directly before his grandmother and his aunt, who saw him last three years back, and tell them that he does not like them. He is fierce. He hates the dirt of this house. He complains at the cobwebs and the spiders. He scolds the animals when they come in, for the dirt that they bring.'

The hens passed through the house, front door to back, as easily as through the courtyard, and a white cockerel liked to perch on the back of the wooden bench in the hall.

Natraj would not eat his grandmother's food. He demanded that his mother make him northern dishes, chappatis and heavy dahls. Most horrifying of all to him was the kitchen, a black hellhole at the back of the house with a clay stove that burnt wood or cow dung. The smoke was supposed to escape through a rough vent between the roof tiles and the walls bore a decade's soot. Maya said that her father had spoken of whitewashing it yearly. Since he had died, even the possibility had faded away.

To make coffee, she kindled a fire of casuarina twigs. During the rains, when even the air was saturated with moisture, the fire would take a long time to catch. As the milk warmed she squatted on a wooden stool a couple of inches above the beaten earth floor. Once I commented on how supple she was, squatting, bending to place wood in the fire, rising without a pause, despite her belly, to rinse a cup at the well.

'No, I am weak. Village women must be strong. Last time I was as strong as my sister-in-law, who keeps up all the work though her baby is due a week before mine, lifting, grinding rice.'

Maya made our coffee cup by cup, mixing warmed milk and coffee by pouring it from cup to bowl and back again, tipping sugar into the cup from the palm of her hand and mixing again.

'At Jamshedpur we have a gas cooker, four rings. And we have running water. A meal can be cooked in half an hour, using the rings

185

together. Then a woman has time to sew, knit, work on other things. In Jamshedpur winters are cold and my neighbours have taught me how to knit. Sometimes we must wear three sweaters, hats and gloves.'

Natraj complained about the heat in the south. Why were there mosquitoes here, he asked, when there were no mosquitoes at home? His legs were a mass of red bites. He scratched them constantly and pulled at the dirty cotton bandage on his knee.

Natraj's father was a native of Porayar, his parents born barely two kilometres apart. At Jamshedpur he was growing up in a compound that was shared with six other families and not one of them was Tamil. Seven states were represented there and at least that many languages: Hindi and English, Bengali, Malayalam, Tamil, Punjabi (there was one Sikh family, the only non-Hindus), Bihari and Gujarati. As the address, Traffic Colony, suggested, all the men worked on the railways. The community was close. The neighbours had to support one another since all had been uprooted from village and extended family. But the society they formed was bound to be different from those they had left, where identities and relationships were known and set for generations.

Natraj came to our house with a touch of snobbery and played with the few toys we had brought out for Tom. He was knowing when presented with a miniature double-decker bus. Those he had seen in Calcutta.

It was Maya who told me about the goddess Angalaman, one of the seven sisters of Mariamman and as terrible, a black goddess in a black sari.

Maya defined her as a non-vegetarian god, the classification sounding banal in Indian-English. It meant that her devotees and her priests or pujaris were of low, non-vegetarian castes, and that unlike the gods of the brahmins she did not shy from animal sacrifice. Angalaman and her sisters were ancient goddesses, female like most of India's village deities. They probably originated in the tribal religion of Dravidian India, before the arrival of the Aryans and the introduction of the brahmin religion. When brahminism did take hold, it did not deny the Dravidian gods but absorbed them into the Hindu pantheon, and sometimes anthropomorphised them, when they were no more than animistic forces, so that they gained a form like that of a Hindu god. So the old religion had come to underlie the brahmin superstructure. Village shrines remained in addition to brahmin temples. While those temples were associated with the hierarchy of caste, and in earlier times with royal dynasties, the village shrine and the village deity continued to be the focus for the rural communities.

Angalaman is known as a goddess throughout Tamil Nadu. The major characteristics ascribed to her are anger and a greed for bones. To appease her, Tranquebar, like other villages in the region, celebrates an annual festival in her honour.

Maya told me that that year's celebration had begun the previous night, when a man had performed a dance with a pot of flowers on his head. In the morning a terracotta firepot had been carried in procession around the houses of the village. I remembered when she spoke of it that I had heard drumming pass down the street, early, as we were getting up. Hindus, and also Christians and Muslims, put oil and money in the pot and marked their faces with a streak of charcoal that signified that their offering had won the goddess's protection for their household through the following year. The festival was to reach its climax with a third ritual, a dance, on the following night.

We talked in the inner room where Maya and the children slept. Maya's brother came in and sat himself cross-legged on the corner of a table. He said that Angalaman's festival wasn't a patch on Mariamman's, which took place in April or May and drew lakhs of pilgrims coming on foot from Nagore, Nagapattinam, Karikal, miles around. That I should stay to see.

He told how most of Mariamman's pilgrims come as a result of a specific fear or debt: one of their family may have contracted one of the diseases with which she is associated, or they themselves have recovered from it. A large proportion are fishing people or members of the builder's caste, for whom she has a special significance. They usually fast in some way before the festival, perhaps simply abstaining from fish, meat and eggs for five consecutive Sundays (he was precise, as a Hindu will be, on the details of the religious observance) and they bring offerings of money, a theoretically propitious sum

187

such as fifty-one, a hundred and one, two hundred and one rupees. The festival is a huge carnival. Most of the pilgrims wear yellow, Mariamman's colour, but among them are men dressed as tigers and other animals, and pilgrims who 'take covadi', performing ritual mortification. Around the covadi, the others drum, sing and dance, making offerings and showering them with water.

I asked about that expression, covadi. He explained how people make a vow to Mariamman or to some other god that they will honour them, for a designated period of one, three, seven years or more, by attending their festival with their tongues transfixed by metal rods or their bodies stuck with needles. Again, he gave precise requirements. Rods may be inserted through tongues alone or curved through both cheeks. Either a hundred and one or a hundred and eight is a good number for the needles, the tips of which can be decorated with flowers, limes, or even electric light bulbs attached to a power source.

He had seen men prepare before the Mariamman festival. The subject, in a trance, chants the goddess's name. Another rubs his skin with ash powder and then inserts the needles or rods, which may simply be sharpened spokes from umbrellas or bicycle wheels. He said that though in ordinary life the needles would draw blood straightaway, there is none at festival time. And when the rods are removed and the skin is rubbed with flowers and sandal paste, again there is no blood and there is no scarring.

I asked, 'Do you know anyone who has taken covadi?'

'There is a man, Kandan, a fisherman, lives at the end of this street, in one of the fishing huts, the fourth or fifth along by the gaol bungalow. He has taken covadi for nineteen years. He is a very poor man, so he comes to all the houses along this street to collect money. Some twenty to twenty-five years ago he had a period of bad luck and many illnesses. Then he made the vow to Mariamman to take covadi each year as long as he lived. Now he is in his mid-fifties, a very small man but strong. He has five or six children.'

'It is the poor people who pray like this,' Maya added. 'Richer people can give money. The poor man can offer only a vow. Some say they will visit seven places, seven towns, and collect money in the streets. For beggars this is easy, but for ordinary people, people

188

who work for money, it is difficult. They bathe at the tank and go in wet clothes, carrying a dish with nim leaves. They say they will do puja for Mariamman and collect paise, rice and fruit which they will give to the god.'

28

On the night of the Angalaman dance, Regina Mary came to stay with Tom. I offered her a bed but she preferred to sleep on the floor. She liked the cool of its stone tiles.

Maya sent a friend to escort me since she said the dance was frightening. Edwin was a Christian, a jobless graduate who bred chickens in the yard before his snowy white hut, a neat and diffident fellow who shared his veranda with chicks that were caged beneath basketwork domes and had their feathers dyed pink or yellow according to gender. He had never seen the dance before. He came in jeans, gold cross at his neck, shoulders shawled in a towel that bore a print of red carnations. The dress was suitable for the night's relative cold but it made him look, with his black moustache, more Mexican than Indian, so that even a rampaging god might distinguish him from a Hindu.

At midnight we went to Angalaman's temple. Others besides ourselves were out on the village streets, pairs walking with soft steps, bodies stirring on verandas, shrouded forms asleep on the ground along the route the dance would take. The temple lay in the north of the village close to the shore, on the borderline between the colonial and fishing settlements. Before it was a small open space that had been lit for the occasion by fluorescent tubes suspended between poles. People had begun to gather there, restless feet churning up the bright dust. At the edge of the glare a dozen children slept head to foot, cloths drawn over their faces.

The temple was a plain concrete building, flat-roofed behind a parapet of Chinese curlicues. The structure was modern though there had been an Angalaman temple on the site for well over a century; ritual demanded that it was rebuilt every twelve years. Inside, the gods too were modern, crudely made and garishly painted. Angalaman's six subordinates grimaced from niches in the side walls, bulbous-eyed figures brandishing knives in their multiple hands. The most hideous held in her lap the bodies of a woman and baby, both disembowelled, and dangled spaghetti entrails from bloody lips. Beneath her right foot lay the crushed figure of a man.

The niches were cluttered with rags and discarded bottles of anointing oil. The floor was unswept, even in the sanctuary where the idol of the goddess stood. In a brahmin temple the sanctuary is sacred ground, entered only by gliding male priests in the ritual dress of sacred thread and white dhoti. Here the black-draped Angalaman was tended by women and there was nothing hieratic in their appearance. They were dark, Dravidian looking, dressed in clashing saris of orange and black and pink. Among them was a tall bold girl whom I knew as the daughter of the temple's priest.

The girl told us a story of Angalaman's power. Edwin translated. Once there was a wicked king N—, who so oppressed his people that they called on Angalaman for help. The queen was pregnant, about to give birth to the king's first child. No doctor, no midwife, no nurse was to be found. Angalaman's deputy appeared before the palace gates in the guise of an old woman, a midwife, and she was entrusted with the birth. So she went to the queen as she was in labour and ripped the baby out from her belly, then put her teeth to it and tore out its intestines. When queen and baby were dead, she cast the king to the ground and crushed him beneath her feet.

The girl's deep voice beat out the rhythm of the Tamil. She told the horrid tale with animation. Angalaman was indeed a carnivorous and angry goddess, one who must be propitiated, but by this story, one whose cruelty avenged those who worshipped her.

'Come! Come!' The girl's smile was wide and elated. Round the back of the temple, in a room like a stable, the dancers were being made up. Her father the priest was sick and her brother was to take part for the first time. He was a teenager, a slim boy without his sister's forceful features. He sat like stone as his face was painted gleaming black (his dressers using up a dozen shallow cosmetic pots) and also his hands and arms, his neck and upper chest. Lines of fine white dots were applied to define his eyes and mouth. Three other men were made up beside him, their faces painted in swirls of dark colour. The room was hot, crowded, the door closed to keep out

191

spectators whose faces pressed against the barred window. When the dressers paused, the priest's son looked vulnerable, separated from the rest. His face was fixed with concentration. He turned it to the wall. In his bare back, brown to the shoulderblades, black above, the muscles were taut.

The trappings of the god-dancer lay in the courtyard: a head-dress shaped like a bishop's mitre, coated with black hair and decorated with gold thread and rosettes of sequins, with thick twisted braids dangling five foot to reach to the wearer's ankles; a black bodice; a skirt like a grass skirt but made of thin strips of black cloth attached to a string that wound a few times around the waist; a trident with a lemon on its central prong; and a pair of huge fangs made of papier mâché and wrapped with gold foil.

At the temple, the priest himself came to watch the dance. His family, builders by caste and by trade, had served Angalaman for four generations. He was a striking man, long boned. He sat limp with fever on the threshold of the sanctuary, sweat breaking on his face and on his lean bare chest.

'A brahmin would not come near this temple,' said someone in the crowd. 'A brahmin would be afraid. It takes a bold man.'

Someone else said how the villagers themselves could be scared of Angalaman's priest: they believed that at times, if only for moments, the priest took on the personality of the god.

There was bravado among the gang of men who waited in the temple. The doors to the outside had been barred. The three drummers who were to play for the dance circled about, giving their drums tense, experimental taps.

One of the drummers was the fisherman Kandan, the coradi from Maya's street. He was a small man, well under five foot with a slight but muscular frame, wiry grey-black hair and a wedge of beard on his chin, goatish. He was proud of the feats he had performed for Mariamman: nineteen times, a hundred and one needles all over his body, one rod through his tongue. Three days fasting beforehand, lying on his stomach, and not a twinge of pain. He put out his tongue as far as it would go. Neither the tongue nor his limbs or bare torso showed any mark save the inoculation scar high on his left arm.

The milling crowd suddenly focused as three of the participants swept into the room. They wore lungis gathered and tied with string to resemble full skirts (Angalaman's chaotic sidekicks female like her incarnations) and clown hats above their grotesquely painted faces, one of straw, one of leather, one a towelling turban. But it was a false start. They were gone in a moment, having grabbed a handful of garish cottons from a chest by the wall – last-minute stuffing for the substitute dancer's hastily fitted head-dress.

Then the drums began in earnest: three different drums, Kandan's small, high pitched and insistent, the others progressively deeper in tone, opening independently and working towards the rhythm of invocation. The drummers' eyes were hectic with drink or fervour, their hands disciplined. As the tempo accelerated one of the crowd grew aggressive, and apparently taking objection to one of the drummers, pranced forward, fixed him in the eye and tried to conduct him to another beat. The drummer defied him – or perhaps he just did not see, closed in on the sound. Though the man was calmed his threat stayed in the air.

Edwin started beside me as the figure of the god-dancer filled the door. He entered with a clumsy leap. The tall head-dress shook and the clowns ran to support it. The boy had yet to learn how to balance its weight. One by one, other men were moved and broke into dance. At some point I became aware of a strange smell, that had entered the room as the dance began and grew fouler and more pervasive. The black figure gathered strength. The smell was suddenly gagging as one of the clowns brought out a winnowing tray piled with pink viscera. They were the entrails of a goat that had been sacrificed three days before. The dancer gripped the golden fangs between his teeth and thrust them into the tray, tangling the entrails about them.

Edwin shouted in my ear. The dance was a representation of the tale told by the priest's daughter.

The drumming reverberated off concrete walls and floor and low ceiling until it seemed the room could barely contain the pressure. When the doors were opened, the dance burst on to the village.

The Angalaman figure lunged at the gathered villagers, a black swirling giant with the rubbery guts dangling from its mouth. It danced with huge unpredictable leaps, forwards or sideways, landing with a clash of anklet bells. The villagers screamed and scattered to

193

escape its touch. The clowns circled it, leading it on, goading it to new jumps. They went round and round the square before the temple, before the white bars of the fluorescent lights – these briefly eclipsed behind the god-dancer and momentarily blinding when he had passed. With an erratic progress, sometimes reversing without warning, the dance drew away from the temple towards the bottom of Goldsmith Street. At the corner was a big crowd. As the black figure jumped, the crowd split and the two sides recoiled like waves on sand. Most of those on the street were men. Women and children pressed over the railings of narrow verandas where their excited faces and the hot colours of saris were picked up by light from indoors. It was a great and terrifying game. They called to the god-dancer and threw him paise but shrank back against the walls if he approached.

At points the drumming ceased and the dancer would rest, propped against a wall. One clown held him up and the others fussed around him, fanned him as he gasped for breath. At those moments, with the drums stopped, reason could detach itself to recognise the mesmeric power of their sound, on spectators as well as participants. After an hour or more, by the tea stall at the junction of Queen and Mosque Streets, I found myself close to the dancer in one such interval. The black paint was greasy with sweat, smeared at the brow; it seemed a rubber mask behind which the face had shrunk away.

The tea-drinkers had seen it before. For a moment they stood back like theatre-goers. A pity, one said, that the boy did not have the strength of his father, who had performed the dance for decades with rarely ever a halt. Yes, said another. If only he was more like his sister. Or if she had been the boy. What an Angalaman she would have made.

But when the drums set up again they fell silent, gripped once more like the rest of us.

The clowns urged the boy back into the dance, the first commanding, the next cajoling, then all three calling in unison. His body hung back until the split second when the spirit – or his trance – returned. As if a hand had picked up the strings of the black puppet, he made a giant leap, throwing people before his path and scattering black shadows across the street.

The last wave of energy came before the fisherman's temple. Beyond, where the street dissolved among the fishing huts, the crowd thinned. The path led to the cremation and burial ground at the edge of the village. Many of the men and all of the women save myself turned back. I was invited to stay, though by Hindu custom women may not go to the cremation ground as they may not follow the body at funerals. The dance had slowed, the drums no more than pulsing down the track between the thorn fences and fishing huts, our passage lit only by a storm lantern carried up ahead. In one yard, an old woman watched. The earth, the mud walls of her hut and her face were monochrome at the farthest reach of the lantern's light.

The track continued between thorn bushes, beyond the village. We passed the entrance to the cremation ground. The god-dancer might not enter by the same route as he would return, so we must use a rough second entrance further on. The dance had ceased altogether. The dancer was supported now on the shoulders of two clowns. His legs dragged and they sang to urge him forward.

The cremation ground was wide, its earth uneven over mounds and hollows of random burials. The dust was deep, spilling warm and soft against the feet. At four a.m. it could have been the heart of a moor, the bare expanse ringed by a thin layer of cloud that separated it from the stars. At its edge rose the utilitarian outline of the concrete incinerator. Some way before that, the dancers stopped. The storm lantern placed on the ground at the centre of the group cast their long shadows out like the spokes of a wheel.

At the place where they stood, the earth had been moulded into the form of a prostrate body representing the king of the Angalaman story. Where the head would have been was a small tin vessel containing a bag of bones. Kandan took them out and showed them to me, small pieces of bone like knuckles. I reached out, but recoiled from touching them. I regretted this later; the hard feel of bone would have supported my memory of what I saw.

The limp body of the god-dancer was let slip to the ground. Fingers opened his mouth so that the entrails could be disgorged on to the tray. Kandan had to tear at them to disentangle the golden fangs. The smell was close again and drew a cloud of flies. Then the men heaved up his reluctant limbs so that he sat astride the dust body.

195

Was the boy inside conscious, in these moments of exhaustion? His eyes suggested delirium. The men squatted before him and coaxed him to open his lips to take the first white bone in his mouth. His jaw moved, slowly, then the energy returned to him and he chewed and the bone crunched between his teeth.

I did not think it should have been possible. I wondered if the bones had been baked or prepared beforehand, but they looked like any other bones.

His mouth was dry and at first he could not swallow. One man stroked his throat and then his chest as if to help the crumbs down, then slipped a second piece into his mouth. The symbolism must be complete: Angalaman's likeness crushing every last piece of the sacrificial victim. It took minutes for each bone to go down, as the boy's teeth ground away and chalky slivers stuck to his lips.

As he swallowed the last, the participants turned on the onlookers and chased us away. For this critical stage of the ritual, as the spirit departed, no other person must touch him. I watched from a distance as they rolled him over on the ground and cast sand over his body, the struggle of their shadows vast and indecipherable. At last they rose, the boy too, and slunk back towards the village. By the door of a house on the outskirts they threw themselves on the ground to wait until daylight, when they must dance back to the temple.

At seven I heard their drums. I went out carrying Tom, looked down the sunlit street. The milkman cycled by, brass churn glinting, as the tired dancers turned down Goldsmith Street. The images did not connect, the figures from the night like strays in the waking day. It was the builder's son in fancy dress.

29

Every day I must have passed the Nadar house on King Street. My first impression had been of a men's club. There had been the slow talk drifting between the veranda columns, the white figures slung across the benches outside the open doors or, in the mornings when the shadows of the columns striped the floor, on the sloping chairs within. But that impression must have dated from the week we arrived at Tranquebar, around the time the man there died of chickenpox. Male relations and friends gathered then to see his death through.

What I first knew of the building was the colonial identity: eighteenth century, neoclassical, last European occupant a man named Van Theylingen who died in 1873 – it may have changed hands at least once after that before the Nadars bought it. Later this identity became submerged beneath my knowledge of the family and of the recent tragic intervention of Mariamman.

I had had the story of the young man's death from a Lutheran pastoress and then from a brahmin doctor. It had offended them equally. Both judged that a life had been wasted, one blaming superstition, the other ignorance. I heard the story a third time in the house itself.

We sat in the hall. The two children of the dead man clambered over the arms of my wooden settee. I knew who they were, having once encountered them with their grandmother at the Chandrasekarans' and shared an auto home. The boy was four, the girl two, chubby and bud mouthed. There was a man visiting, a cousin from Porayar, who told me anyway: 'Their father is expired.' The statement was colourless, the word a trifle absurd, derived from the English of official documents and not of feeling.

The hall was a square room, made rich by the emerald green of the dado below the whitewash – the same colour as was fading in the sunlight that penetrated the veranda. It was formally arranged. The settee faced the doors to the street and the tall windows set into the arches beside them. Narrow console tables, ornately carved and supporting long mirrors, faced one another on the side walls where the light from the windows slanted oilily across. Beside them, double doors led symmetrically to the two wings of the house. One pair was padlocked as the rooms to the east and those on the upper floor belonged to a brother absent in Madras. The others were open. On the threshold stood the mother of the dead man, a fine-looking woman whose hair was grey but whose skin was still smooth.

It was she who ran the house, who took the children to the doctor's and was the public face of the family. The man's widow rarely appeared outside. Consigned to the secondary role of daughter-in-law without any hope of compensatory power as wife – or of escape by remarriage – she stayed in the back and heated Horlicks for the guests.

The visitor made smalltalk and the children looked at a picture book I had brought. All the while a toothless old servant woman squatted opposite me on the floor. When I rose to leave, she pulled at my arm. In Tamil she recounted every incident in the drama. She supported her words in mime, putting fingers to her face to show the spots and the dreadful itching of the disease, then indicating the onset of convulsions and the futility of the doctor's eventual visit. She marked the swift onset of the man's karma with a sweep of the hand and a shrug of loss.

At the Mariamman Temple at Ohruga Mangalam, a family came to picnic. They were middle class: they drove in their own car and the three children wore 'readymades' in synthetic fabrics, the sort of clothes that can be bought only in big towns. The mother laid a mat on the ground just inside the gate of the little country temple. The floor was unswept and there were many insects to be brushed aside. The family settled down noisily to eat the five different dishes she had packed in the tiffin can. Two of the children had got over chicken-pox and the third was out of quarantine.

Mariamman's statue lurked in her shrine, known by the glimmer of yellow from her sari. In the courtyard her festival cars were bright as pinball machines, stuck with pieces of mirror and coloured glass. On the platform beside the gate, a local girl sat before heaps of flowers and threaded garlands, yellow trumpets strung between torn petals of scarlet hibiscus.

By the old port at Tranquebar, before the isolated white building of the fisheries office, cut tree trunks had been unloaded for the making of the new season's catamarans. They were spread in rows across the open ground. Where some lay in shade, a gang of men squatted to rest before beginning the cutting. Women scraped off the bark and carried it away in baskets on their heads.

The fields inland had been shorn of rice. Stacks of cut stalks ringed the threshing platforms and black buffalo dragged harvest carts along the roads. At the junction between the Porayar and Karikal roads they had to skirt a golden roundabout of threshed grain. A small grey kite took off from a telegraph pole nearby with a flash of black wing-tips, wheeled upwards and hovered where some animal was exposed in the stubble.

Late one afternoon at Thaiub Ali's, the girls plucked leaves from the henna bush by the tank and made up a green paste with which to paint our palms. They had prepared in advance a miniature stencil for Tom's hand. We went to the upper room. Every surface smelled of wood: the dark teak of the broad-planked floor, the beams and rafters of the roof (bowed like a ship's hull), the carved bed with its four turned posts for mosquito netting, the desk, the flat swing-seat which hung on chains from a beam, the shutters of the windows on each of the four walls.

The girls placed their flower stencils on our palms and painted them. The windows opened on to greenness, the close foliage of the trees and creepers that embraced the house's half-ruin. We had to keep our hands still as the henna dried and even Tom was still for a time. As the seat swung beneath us, his eyes were drawn to a flickering grid of light low on the wall. It must have been refracted off the water of the tank and again off the shiny leaves. He watched as the sunlight slanted more obliquely and the dancing grid edged away.

*   *   *

199

There were many partings. I went to say goodbye at the post office. The postmaster nodded. 'You are leaving. I know. Your telegram on Monday.'

Wilson brought a gift of two crab shells. He handled them delicately, pointing out their strange markings. 'These are very rare. I myself found them on the sand when I was walking, and I have been keeping them for such an occasion. Take them with my prayers. They will be very important to you and to your husband. See, each shell bears the marks of the cross and of angels.'

The cross ran down the centre of each shell, an albino outline against the pink. To each side of it the shape of an angel could be distinguished, kneeling in profile. The forms were distorted but the markings were almost symmetrical, like an ink smudge across two halves of a folded paper. They were the shells of a certain type of crab, known in India as Xavier shells. There is a story that the Portuguese missionary saint took pity on the crabs, which were preyed upon by many creatures, and gave them the holy markings for their protection. I thought it a pretty legend. To Wilson, the existence of the crab shells was a miracle. From his discovery of them also he seemed to impute divine significance.

Around AD 1347, a Florentine priest named John of Marignolli came to Ceylon and the Coromandel coast; he was returning from China where he had gone as papal legate to the court of the Great Khan. In Ceylon he first saw plantains and he too marvelled at a pattern. 'And this is a thing that I have seen with mine own eyes, that slice it across where you will, you will find on both sides of the cut the figure of a man crucified, as if one had graven it with a needle point.'

It was a minute's walk from the house to the temple on the shore: left past Oudoumane's, across the track that was grandly labelled Post Office Street, and between the old walls that still enclosed the abandoned plots behind the seashore bungalow. Though every brick had gone from the houses that had stood there, the wells remained. Women and children came from the fishing huts to wash, and goats browsed the undergrowth. Often children were to be found at another well just by the temple gate, where the sole remaining house was usually padlocked. It was the priest's house but I never saw him until the last week. The temple was always swept, the gods freshly anointed and garlanded, but silent. A boy might climb over the broken foundations on his way from one beach to another, or there'd be the men panning the mud where the waves pounded at the rubble, or someone gazing out to sea. Then, a few days before I left, I found the house by the gate open and the priest standing before it.

His name was Meenakshi Sundaram and he looked brahmin to his fingertips, a man fine as a sharpened pencil. He was forty-four: grey hair beginning to thin, straight teeth reddened at the edges with pan, light skin smooth beneath the white thread and the streaks of ash on upper arms, stomach and forehead.

The house was pretty much abandoned. The whitewash of the walls inside was greyed and smudged, peeling behind a few printed posters of gods. In the first room a few belongings were kept in two great wooden chests that were raised from the floor, one on bricks, the other on a roughly carpentered pedestal. There were two solid wooden armchairs and a third teetered in the corner with a broken leg. In the second, inner room, brass vessels lay in the dirt.

'Six months back, I moved with my family to my native village of Thirukkalacheri. It was necessary on account of the sea air. It was not healthy to live here. My wife in particular is very sensitive and she is allergic to the air. Even myself, I have had anti-allergenics prescribed.

'Listen.'

The thud of the sea was constant.

'This house is too close to the sea. The other houses in the village stand away from the beach. Breathe here and you breathe in chills, fevers and dysenteries.' He took a yogic breath that travelled visibly to his solar plexus, then expelled it cautiously.

Each morning he cycled from Thirukkalacheri, bringing flowers from his garden for the gods at Tranquebar. He performed puja at this temple and at others in the village, attending the fisherman's temple from half past four to half past five each afternoon. Occasionally, by request, he also performed puja at the Angalaman temple.

'It is not adequate. It is difficult to live as a priest here. A village is not a suitable place for making puja.'

All the men in his family were priests. His grandfather had been

201

priest at Thirukkalacheri, then his father, and now his brother was there. His grandfather's brother, and his descendants, had the temple in the next village. His brother-in-law worked at a small temple in Madras and he had sent his son to live with him there.

'In Madras, the earnings are very suitable. Gurukkal [priest] can become a rich man. My son is a clever boy. He studied for seven years at Thiruvanamalai, learning Sanskrit and reading the Vedas. He has been working at two or three different temples in Madras, one of the hundred priests at the great temple of Vadapalani. He has beautiful hair.'

He stated this like a qualification. A fine black chukra – the topknot worn by the brahmin priest – would get the boy noticed.

The Masila Nather temple at Tranquebar had been built, he said, six hundred and eighty-five years ago by King Kulothongasolan. This was recorded in an inscription on stone, where the village is known by its old name of Sadanganbadi. The stone had now fallen into the sea.

He had watched the temple deteriorate through successive rains. The far wall of the enclosure had been engulfed some thirty-five years before, and with it the shrine of Sarasvati. A replacement shrine had been erected in a space to the back of the cramped courtyard. Twenty years later, another chunk of the temple was lost to the sea. At the same time the well had turned salty. Five lakhs of rupees had recently been sanctioned for the preservation of the temple, but not one had yet been forthcoming because of what he termed local obstacles.

The old walls showed fine workmanship, the masonry even, the carving clean and delicate, the granite scarcely weathered. The priest introduced me to his gods, who glistened black with anointing oil. He produced fresh pink flowers from a little plastic bag that dangled from his hand and placed them on the gods, picking out from the oil as he did so the previous day's wilted offerings.

The central shrine faced on to a ledge barely a yard wide, at the edge of which the paving made its sudden drop to the sea. He unlocked the doors. The morning sun and the sound of the waves broke directly into the chamber, which would originally have been shaded by high surrounding walls. The light was almost shocking

after the accustomed obscurity of Hindu shrines. It seemed a Medi-
terranean room, walls mottled blue, lintels and capitals pink. In the
sanctuary at the end was the lingam of Masila Nather, draped in
white cotton and painted with a yellow dot like a Cyclopean eye; to
its left, a small Ganesh; before it a Nandi, Shiva's bull. Along the side
walls were other idols and stone slabs carved with interlocking
snakes. Among these were some that had been saved as the rest of
the temple was lost.

On the twenty-fifth of March, Meenakshi Sundaram was to audition
for All India Radio. When not doing puja, he sang the ragas of south
India, Carnatic music, at weddings and celebrations. He brought out
a roneoed letter from a thin pink envelope. It invited him for a first
audition as a vocalist at Trichinopoly and regretted that travelling
expenses could not be paid. This would be the first of a series of
auditions in a national talent contest whose winners would be
accorded a recording session in Delhi.

As the weather warmed, the sea was often low, glowing blue, no
more than ruffled by wave crests. One afternoon I spent walking
down the beach, southwards in a straight line right at the water's
edge, past the dry channels where the river used to cross the sand.
The waves sounded coolly on one side, the sun burned on the other.
Sometimes my feet were on sand, sometimes in water as a wave
came in. Ahead, the white scallops of foam formed and re-formed,
and the sand shone where they receded. For an instant as the water
pulled back, mussels lay exposed, flat on the wet sand, finely patterned in bronze and red, until in a motion smooth as that of a wave,
they flicked on their narrow sides to be sucked back beneath the
surface.

Few shells were washed up whole. Yet even a shattered piece can
be beautiful to hold for a moment, suggestive of the original form.
And in a broken shell secret whorls are revealed. They glinted on
the sand, discs of abalone, a black scallop, a tiny perfect shell wedged
within a larger fragment.

After a mile or more there was a fishing village: palms around
palm-thatched huts, black figures swarming among the catamarans
on the strand. Children's yells broke through the air, laughs at the

sight of a foreigner and cries of paise! I turned back along the water-
line. Footprints had disappeared as fast as they were made but the
trail was marked at points by remembered shells that had been
carried for a while and then discarded.

Before the fort gate, cars and a jeep were parked. At home, Regina
Mary had news. There had been a suicide in the fort that morning.
The watchman found the body when he went in around eight o'clock.
Regina Mary saw four men carry it out from the gate when she came
back from lunch. People said that the dead man came from Kathan
Savadi, the village by Porayar where Thaiub Ali had his house, and
that he had taken poison.

Two days later, the Thursday, I was again at Thaiub Ali's. The family
was about to set off for Nagore, where they spent every Thursday
night with relatives so that they could pray at the mosque the next
morning. Though some way off, it had been their family mosque since
Thaiub Ali had experienced its healing power, and later his daughter
too had been cured of an illness during a visit there.

The suicide had been a neighbour. Thaiub Ali drew my attention
to the sound of wailing that came through the trees from the direction
of his home.

'He was the tea-shop owner. Had the tea shop on the crossroads.
His name was Muthukrishnan, a very good, very soft fellow, aged
twenty-two or twenty-four. He had family problems, financial problems: father expired; one no-good brother, a drunk; mother and two
sisters to support as well as this brother. Seven days before he killed
himself, the elder sister was married. It was the loans he took out
for her dowry that broke him.'

'What happens to the family now?'

'No income.' Nothing to speculate about. The facts were plain.

'And the second sister, will she be able to marry?'

'No dowry.'

The Johnsons came to see me. I offered them tea. Johnson, whom
I had seen little, because of illness and then perhaps his shyness,
would have only water. He said he drank nothing but water. He
spoke fast and intensely, his eyes evasive. When he was young he

had made a trip to the north. He saw the poor in Calcutta and he saw the tea gardens. And he made a vow never again to drink tea or coffee. If the labour and money expended on these non-nutritious substances were instead put towards wheat and rice, he had reasoned, the people's poverty might be eradicated. In the thirty years that had passed since, he had not once broken his vow, not even while he lived in Germany and Sweden. Now he kept to it, though he believed that it was a glass of water, hastily gulped at a bus station, that had given him typhoid.

The position of their house gave the Johnsons command of comings and goings at the fort. Suicides such as that of Muthukrishnan were not uncommon, according to Eva Maria. Before coming to Tamil Nadu she had done pastoral work in the German inner city, where she had seen suicide as a modern Western disease. She had been shocked to find it as prevalent in India. Only here the souls of suicides were believed to live on to possess the living. All week the watchman had been afraid to enter the Danish fort.

Next morning we were to leave at nine for the station at Mayuram. At five-thirty, Ismail our water-bearer came with an envelope full of toffees for Tom. It was the same envelope that I had used for his tip, when the new plumbing arrangement had made him redundant a few days before.